This work belongs to
BEERS WERE MADE AND TASTED
FROM
TO
IF YOU FIND THIS, PLEASE RETURN TO

The Home Brewer's Lab Book

My Life in Beer

CHRONICLE BOOKS
SAN FRANCISCO

ISBN 978-1-4521-2351-6

Manufactured in China
Design by Ryan Hayes

10 9 8 7 6 5 4 3 2 1

Chronicle Books LLC
680 Second Street
San Francisco, California 94107
www.chroniclebooks.com

How to use this book

This journal is for you to keep track of how you make beer. By creating this reference for yourself, you will constantly improve your craft, and keep track of all the great beer you make.

Once you've completed this book, look back over what you've recorded. You now have a scientific record of accomplishment, of experimentation, and of creating your perfect brew.

Key Definitions

These systems are used to measure beer intensity, alcohol content, color, and bitterness.

OG ORIGINAL GRAVITY: a measurement of the sucrose in a water-sucrose solution during fermentation; in other words, the amount of sugars in your beer mixture measured using a hydrometer. Measuring original gravity demonstrates how alcoholic your beer is, as well as how much sugar is left for the yeast to consume.

ABV ALCOHOL BY VOLUME: the amount of alcohol measured in terms of volume of alcohol per volume of beer

SRM STANDARD REFERENCE METHOD: a system for measuring the color of your beer, using either a spectrometer or a beer color card

IBU INTERNATIONAL BITTERNESS UNIT: a scale system for measuring the bitterness in beer, usually caused by hops

NAME | TYPE
PROPERTIES I'M GOING FOR
FORM
NOTES
FLAVOR/AROMA/PROCESS

Ingredients

Yeast

NAME

MANUFACTURER

LAST CULTURED

Water

pH TREATMENT ○ YES ○ NO

TYPE

Grain

NAME

ORIGIN

TYPE

ROASTED/TOASTED

○ WHEAT	___%	○ CORN	___%
○ BARLEY	___%	○ OATS	___%
○ MALT	___%	○ RICE	___%
○ RYE	___%	○ OTHER	___%

SPECIFIC PROPERTIES

Hops

VARIETY

SPECIFIC PROPERTIES

% AMOUNT

ORIGIN/NAME

Sugar

GRANULATED SUGAR

BROWN SUGAR

HONEY

MAPLE SYRUP

CORN SYRUP

MALT

MOLASSES

OTHER

Other Flavorings

TYPE

AMOUNT

USED FOR

ADDED DURING

NOTES

Brewing Log

DATE BREWED ______

BATCH SIZE ______

TASTING NOTES ______

BEGINNING SPECIFIC GRAVITY ______

FINAL SPECIFIC GRAVITY ______

______ % ALCOHOL ______

Boil + Mash

TEMPERATURE OF GRAIN ______

TEMPERATURE OF TUN ______

BOIL TIME ______

COOLING TIME & TEMPERATURE ______

Hops added

BOIL TIME ______

COOLING TIME & TEMPERATURE ______

SPECIFIC GRAVITY ______

Yeast added

TEMPERATURE ______

LENGTH OF FERMENT ______

BOTTLING GRAVITY ______

TYPE OF VESSEL ______

PRIMER & AMOUNT ______

Storing and Aging

AGED FOR ______

STORAGE TEMPERATURE ______

NOTES ______

Tasting and Visual Notes

______ OG ______ SRM

______ ABV ______ IBUs

APPEARANCE ______

AROMA ______

FLAVOR ______

FEEL ______

OVERALL ______

WHAT WORKED?

WHAT DIDN'T?

NAME ______ TYPE ______

PROPERTIES I'M GOING FOR ______

FORM ______

NOTES ______

FLAVOR/AROMA/PROCESS ______

Ingredients

Yeast

NAME ______

MANUFACTURER ______

LAST CULTURED ______

Water

pH TREATMENT ○ YES ○ NO

TYPE ______

Grain

NAME ______

ORIGIN ______

TYPE ______

ROASTED/TOASTED ______

○ WHEAT ____% ○ CORN ____%

○ BARLEY ____% ○ OATS ____%

○ MALT ____% ○ RICE ____%

○ RYE ____% ○ OTHER ____%

SPECIFIC PROPERTIES ______

Hops

VARIETY ______

SPECIFIC PROPERTIES ______

% AMOUNT ______

ORIGIN/NAME ______

Sugar

GRANULATED SUGAR ______

BROWN SUGAR ______

HONEY ______

MAPLE SYRUP ______

CORN SYRUP ______

MALT ______

MOLASSES ______

OTHER ______

Other Flavorings

TYPE ______

AMOUNT ______

USED FOR ______

ADDED DURING ______

NOTES ______

Brewing Log

DATE BREWED ________________

BATCH SIZE ________________

TASTING NOTES ________________

____

____

BEGINNING SPECIFIC GRAVITY ________

FINAL SPECIFIC GRAVITY ________

______ % ALCOHOL ________

Boil + Mash

TEMPERATURE OF GRAIN ________________

TEMPERATURE OF TUN ________________

BOIL TIME ________________

COOLING TIME & TEMPERATURE ________________

Hops added

BOIL TIME ________________

COOLING TIME & TEMPERATURE ________________

SPECIFIC GRAVITY ________________

Yeast added

TEMPERATURE ________________

LENGTH OF FERMENT ________________

BOTTLING GRAVITY ________________

TYPE OF VESSEL ________________

PRIMER & AMOUNT ________________

Storing and Aging

AGED FOR ________________

STORAGE TEMPERATURE ________________

NOTES ________________

Tasting and Visual Notes

______ OG ______ SRM

______ ABV ______ IBUs

APPEARANCE ________________

AROMA ________________

FLAVOR ________________

FEEL ________________

OVERALL ________________

WHAT WORKED?

____

WHAT DIDN'T?

____

NAME TYPE
PROPERTIES I'M GOING FOR
FORM
NOTES
FLAVOR/AROMA/PROCESS

Ingredients

Yeast

NAME
MANUFACTURER
LAST CULTURED

Water

pH TREATMENT ○ YES ○ NO
TYPE

Grain

NAME
ORIGIN
TYPE
ROASTED/TOASTED

○ WHEAT	____%	○ CORN	____%
○ BARLEY	____%	○ OATS	____%
○ MALT	____%	○ RICE	____%
○ RYE	____%	○ OTHER	____%

SPECIFIC PROPERTIES

Hops

VARIETY
SPECIFIC PROPERTIES
% AMOUNT
ORIGIN/NAME

Sugar

GRANULATED SUGAR
BROWN SUGAR
HONEY
MAPLE SYRUP
CORN SYRUP
MALT
MOLASSES
OTHER

Other Flavorings

TYPE
AMOUNT
USED FOR
ADDED DURING

NOTES

Brewing Log

DATE BREWED ______

BATCH SIZE ______

TASTING NOTES ______

______

______

BEGINNING SPECIFIC GRAVITY ______

FINAL SPECIFIC GRAVITY ______

______ % ALCOHOL ______

Boil + Mash

TEMPERATURE OF GRAIN ______

TEMPERATURE OF TUN ______

BOIL TIME ______

COOLING TIME & TEMPERATURE ______

Hops added

BOIL TIME ______

COOLING TIME & TEMPERATURE ______

SPECIFIC GRAVITY ______

Yeast added

TEMPERATURE ______

LENGTH OF FERMENT ______

BOTTLING GRAVITY ______

TYPE OF VESSEL ______

PRIMER & AMOUNT ______

Storing and Aging

AGED FOR ______

STORAGE TEMPERATURE ______

NOTES ______

Tasting and Visual Notes

______ OG ______ SRM

______ ABV ______ IBUs

APPEARANCE ______

AROMA ______

FLAVOR ______

FEEL ______

OVERALL ______

WHAT WORKED?

______

WHAT DIDN'T?

______

NAME ______ TYPE ______
PROPERTIES I'M GOING FOR ______
FORM ______
NOTES ______
FLAVOR/AROMA/PROCESS ______

Ingredients

Yeast

NAME ______
MANUFACTURER ______
LAST CULTURED ______

Water

pH TREATMENT ○ YES ○ NO
TYPE ______

Grain

NAME ______
ORIGIN ______
TYPE ______
ROASTED/TOASTED ______

- ○ WHEAT ____%
- ○ BARLEY ____%
- ○ MALT ____%
- ○ RYE ____%
- ○ CORN ____%
- ○ OATS ____%
- ○ RICE ____%
- ○ OTHER ____%

SPECIFIC PROPERTIES ______

Hops

VARIETY ______
SPECIFIC PROPERTIES ______
% AMOUNT ______
ORIGIN/NAME ______

Sugar

GRANULATED SUGAR ______
BROWN SUGAR ______
HONEY ______
MAPLE SYRUP ______
CORN SYRUP ______
MALT ______
MOLASSES ______
OTHER ______

Other Flavorings

TYPE ______
AMOUNT ______
USED FOR ______
ADDED DURING ______

NOTES ______

Brewing Log

DATE BREWED ______________________

BATCH SIZE ______________________

TASTING NOTES ______________________

____

____

BEGINNING SPECIFIC GRAVITY __________

FINAL SPECIFIC GRAVITY __________

______ % ALCOHOL __________

Boil + Mash

TEMPERATURE OF GRAIN ______________

TEMPERATURE OF TUN ______________

BOIL TIME ______________

COOLING TIME & TEMPERATURE ______________

Hops added

BOIL TIME ______________

COOLING TIME & TEMPERATURE ______________

SPECIFIC GRAVITY ______________

Yeast added

TEMPERATURE ______________

LENGTH OF FERMENT ______________

BOTTLING GRAVITY ______________

TYPE OF VESSEL ______________

PRIMER & AMOUNT ______________

Storing and Aging

AGED FOR ______________

STORAGE TEMPERATURE ______________

NOTES ______________________

Tasting and Visual Notes

______ OG ______ SRM

______ ABV ______ IBUs

APPEARANCE ______________________

AROMA ______________________

FLAVOR ______________________

FEEL ______________________

OVERALL ______________________

WHAT WORKED?

____

____

____

WHAT DIDN'T?

____

____

____

NAME | TYPE

PROPERTIES I'M GOING FOR

FORM

NOTES

FLAVOR/AROMA/PROCESS

Ingredients

Yeast

NAME ____________

MANUFACTURER ____________

LAST CULTURED ____________

Water

pH TREATMENT ○ YES ○ NO

TYPE ____________

Grain

NAME ____________

ORIGIN ____________

TYPE ____________

ROASTED/TOASTED ____________

○ WHEAT ____ % ○ CORN ____ %

○ BARLEY ____ % ○ OATS ____ %

○ MALT ____ % ○ RICE ____ %

○ RYE ____ % ○ OTHER ____ %

SPECIFIC PROPERTIES ____________

Hops

VARIETY ____________

SPECIFIC PROPERTIES ____________

% AMOUNT ____________

ORIGIN/NAME ____________

Sugar

GRANULATED SUGAR ____________

BROWN SUGAR ____________

HONEY ____________

MAPLE SYRUP ____________

CORN SYRUP ____________

MALT ____________

MOLASSES ____________

OTHER ____________

Other Flavorings

TYPE ____________

AMOUNT ____________

USED FOR ____________

ADDED DURING ____________

NOTES ____________

Brewing Log

DATE BREWED ______

BATCH SIZE ______

TASTING NOTES ______

BEGINNING SPECIFIC GRAVITY ______

FINAL SPECIFIC GRAVITY ______

______ % ALCOHOL ______

Boil + Mash

TEMPERATURE OF GRAIN ______

TEMPERATURE OF TUN ______

BOIL TIME ______

COOLING TIME & TEMPERATURE ______

Hops added

BOIL TIME ______

COOLING TIME & TEMPERATURE ______

SPECIFIC GRAVITY ______

Yeast added

TEMPERATURE ______

LENGTH OF FERMENT ______

BOTTLING GRAVITY ______

TYPE OF VESSEL ______

PRIMER & AMOUNT ______

Storing and Aging

AGED FOR ______

STORAGE TEMPERATURE ______

NOTES ______

Tasting and Visual Notes

______ OG ______ SRM

______ ABV ______ IBUs

APPEARANCE ______

AROMA ______

FLAVOR ______

FEEL ______

OVERALL ______

WHAT WORKED?

WHAT DIDN'T?

NAME ______ TYPE ______

PROPERTIES I'M GOING FOR ______

FORM ______

NOTES ______

FLAVOR/AROMA/PROCESS ______

Ingredients

Yeast

NAME ______

MANUFACTURER ______

LAST CULTURED ______

Water

pH TREATMENT ○ YES ○ NO

TYPE ______

Grain

NAME ______

ORIGIN ______

TYPE ______

ROASTED/TOASTED ______

○ WHEAT ___% ○ CORN ___%

○ BARLEY ___% ○ OATS ___%

○ MALT ___% ○ RICE ___%

○ RYE ___% ○ OTHER ___%

SPECIFIC PROPERTIES ______

Hops

VARIETY ______

SPECIFIC PROPERTIES ______

% AMOUNT ______

ORIGIN/NAME ______

Sugar

GRANULATED SUGAR ______

BROWN SUGAR ______

HONEY ______

MAPLE SYRUP ______

CORN SYRUP ______

MALT ______

MOLASSES ______

OTHER ______

Other Flavorings

TYPE ______

AMOUNT ______

USED FOR ______

ADDED DURING ______

NOTES ______

Brewing Log

DATE BREWED ______

BATCH SIZE ______

TASTING NOTES ______

BEGINNING SPECIFIC GRAVITY ______

FINAL SPECIFIC GRAVITY ______

______ % ALCOHOL ______

Boil + Mash

TEMPERATURE OF GRAIN ______

TEMPERATURE OF TUN ______

BOIL TIME ______

COOLING TIME & TEMPERATURE ______

Hops added

BOIL TIME ______

COOLING TIME & TEMPERATURE ______

SPECIFIC GRAVITY ______

Yeast added

TEMPERATURE ______

LENGTH OF FERMENT ______

BOTTLING GRAVITY ______

TYPE OF VESSEL ______

PRIMER & AMOUNT ______

Storing and Aging

AGED FOR ______

STORAGE TEMPERATURE ______

NOTES ______

Tasting and Visual Notes

______ OG ______ SRM

______ ABV ______ IBUs

APPEARANCE ______

AROMA ______

FLAVOR ______

FEEL ______

OVERALL ______

WHAT WORKED?

WHAT DIDN'T?

NAME ______ TYPE ______
PROPERTIES I'M GOING FOR ______
______
FORM ______
NOTES ______
______
FLAVOR/AROMA/PROCESS ______

Ingredients

Yeast

NAME ______
MANUFACTURER ______
LAST CULTURED ______

Water

pH TREATMENT ○ YES ○ NO
TYPE ______

Grain

NAME ______
ORIGIN ______
TYPE ______
ROASTED/TOASTED ______

○ WHEAT ____% ○ CORN ____%
○ BARLEY ____% ○ OATS ____%
○ MALT ____% ○ RICE ____%
○ RYE ____% ○ OTHER ____%

SPECIFIC PROPERTIES ______

Hops

VARIETY ______
SPECIFIC PROPERTIES ______
______
______
% AMOUNT ______
ORIGIN/NAME ______

Sugar

GRANULATED SUGAR ______
BROWN SUGAR ______
HONEY ______
MAPLE SYRUP ______
CORN SYRUP ______
MALT ______
MOLASSES ______
OTHER ______

Other Flavorings

TYPE ______
AMOUNT ______
USED FOR ______
ADDED DURING ______

NOTES ______
______
______
______
______
______
______

Brewing Log

DATE BREWED ______

BATCH SIZE ______

TASTING NOTES ______

BEGINNING SPECIFIC GRAVITY ______

FINAL SPECIFIC GRAVITY ______

______ % ALCOHOL ______

Boil + Mash

TEMPERATURE OF GRAIN ______

TEMPERATURE OF TUN ______

BOIL TIME ______

COOLING TIME & TEMPERATURE ______

Hops added

BOIL TIME ______

COOLING TIME & TEMPERATURE ______

SPECIFIC GRAVITY ______

Yeast added

TEMPERATURE ______

LENGTH OF FERMENT ______

BOTTLING GRAVITY ______

TYPE OF VESSEL ______

PRIMER & AMOUNT ______

Storing and Aging

AGED FOR ______

STORAGE TEMPERATURE ______

NOTES ______

Tasting and Visual Notes

______ OG ______ SRM

______ ABV ______ IBUs

APPEARANCE ______

AROMA ______

FLAVOR ______

FEEL ______

OVERALL ______

WHAT WORKED?

WHAT DIDN'T?

NAME ______ TYPE ______

PROPERTIES I'M GOING FOR ______

FORM ______

NOTES ______

FLAVOR/AROMA/PROCESS ______

Ingredients

Yeast

NAME ______

MANUFACTURER ______

LAST CULTURED ______

Water

pH TREATMENT ○ YES ○ NO

TYPE ______

Grain

NAME ______

ORIGIN ______

TYPE ______

ROASTED/TOASTED ______

○ WHEAT ____% ○ CORN ____%

○ BARLEY ____% ○ OATS ____%

○ MALT ____% ○ RICE ____%

○ RYE ____% ○ OTHER ____%

SPECIFIC PROPERTIES ______

Hops

VARIETY ______

SPECIFIC PROPERTIES ______

% AMOUNT ______

ORIGIN/NAME ______

Sugar

GRANULATED SUGAR ______

BROWN SUGAR ______

HONEY ______

MAPLE SYRUP ______

CORN SYRUP ______

MALT ______

MOLASSES ______

OTHER ______

Other Flavorings

TYPE ______

AMOUNT ______

USED FOR ______

ADDED DURING ______

NOTES ______

Brewing Log

DATE BREWED ____________________

BATCH SIZE ____________________

TASTING NOTES ____________________

BEGINNING SPECIFIC GRAVITY ________

FINAL SPECIFIC GRAVITY ________

______ % ALCOHOL ________

Boil + Mash

TEMPERATURE OF GRAIN ________

TEMPERATURE OF TUN ________

BOIL TIME ________

COOLING TIME & TEMPERATURE ________

Hops added

BOIL TIME ________

COOLING TIME & TEMPERATURE ________

SPECIFIC GRAVITY ________

Yeast added

TEMPERATURE ________

LENGTH OF FERMENT ________

BOTTLING GRAVITY ________

TYPE OF VESSEL ________

PRIMER & AMOUNT ________

Storing and Aging

AGED FOR ________

STORAGE TEMPERATURE ________

NOTES ____________________

Tasting and Visual Notes

______ OG ______ SRM

______ ABV ______ IBUs

APPEARANCE ____________________

AROMA ____________________

FLAVOR ____________________

FEEL ____________________

OVERALL ____________________

WHAT WORKED?

WHAT DIDN'T?

NAME ____ TYPE ____
PROPERTIES I'M GOING FOR ____
FORM ____
NOTES ____
FLAVOR/AROMA/PROCESS ____

Ingredients

Yeast

NAME ____
MANUFACTURER ____
LAST CULTURED ____

Water

pH TREATMENT ○ YES ○ NO
TYPE ____

Grain

NAME ____
ORIGIN ____
TYPE ____
ROASTED/TOASTED ____

○ WHEAT ____% ○ CORN ____%
○ BARLEY ____% ○ OATS ____%
○ MALT ____% ○ RICE ____%
○ RYE ____% ○ OTHER ____%

SPECIFIC PROPERTIES ____

Hops

VARIETY ____
SPECIFIC PROPERTIES ____
% AMOUNT ____
ORIGIN/NAME ____

Sugar

GRANULATED SUGAR ____
BROWN SUGAR ____
HONEY ____
MAPLE SYRUP ____
CORN SYRUP ____
MALT ____
MOLASSES ____
OTHER ____

Other Flavorings

TYPE ____
AMOUNT ____
USED FOR ____
ADDED DURING ____

NOTES ____

Brewing Log

DATE BREWED ______
BATCH SIZE ______
TASTING NOTES ______

BEGINNING SPECIFIC GRAVITY ______
FINAL SPECIFIC GRAVITY ______
______ % ALCOHOL ______

Boil + Mash

TEMPERATURE OF GRAIN ______
TEMPERATURE OF TUN ______
BOIL TIME ______
COOLING TIME & TEMPERATURE ______

Hops added

BOIL TIME ______
COOLING TIME & TEMPERATURE ______
SPECIFIC GRAVITY ______

Yeast added

TEMPERATURE ______
LENGTH OF FERMENT ______
BOTTLING GRAVITY ______
TYPE OF VESSEL ______
PRIMER & AMOUNT ______

Storing and Aging

AGED FOR ______
STORAGE TEMPERATURE ______

NOTES ______

Tasting and Visual Notes

______ OG ______ SRM
______ ABV ______ IBUs

APPEARANCE ______
AROMA ______
FLAVOR ______
FEEL ______
OVERALL ______

WHAT WORKED?

WHAT DIDN'T?

NAME TYPE

PROPERTIES I'M GOING FOR

FORM

NOTES

FLAVOR/AROMA/PROCESS

Ingredients

Yeast

NAME

MANUFACTURER

LAST CULTURED

Water

pH TREATMENT YES NO

TYPE

Grain

NAME

ORIGIN

TYPE

ROASTED/TOASTED

WHEAT ___%

CORN ___%

BARLEY ___%

OATS ___%

MALT ___%

RICE ___%

RYE ___%

OTHER ___%

SPECIFIC PROPERTIES

Hops

VARIETY

SPECIFIC PROPERTIES

% AMOUNT

ORIGIN/NAME

Sugar

GRANULATED SUGAR

BROWN SUGAR

HONEY

MAPLE SYRUP

CORN SYRUP

MALT

MOLASSES

OTHER

Other Flavorings

TYPE

AMOUNT

USED FOR

ADDED DURING

NOTES

Brewing Log

DATE BREWED ______

BATCH SIZE ______

TASTING NOTES ______

______

______

BEGINNING SPECIFIC GRAVITY ______

FINAL SPECIFIC GRAVITY ______

______ % ALCOHOL ______

Boil + Mash

TEMPERATURE OF GRAIN ______

TEMPERATURE OF TUN ______

BOIL TIME ______

COOLING TIME & TEMPERATURE ______

Hops added

BOIL TIME ______

COOLING TIME & TEMPERATURE ______

SPECIFIC GRAVITY ______

Yeast added

TEMPERATURE ______

LENGTH OF FERMENT ______

BOTTLING GRAVITY ______

TYPE OF VESSEL ______

PRIMER & AMOUNT ______

Storing and Aging

AGED FOR ______

STORAGE TEMPERATURE ______

NOTES ______

Tasting and Visual Notes

______ OG ______ SRM

______ ABV ______ IBUs

APPEARANCE ______

AROMA ______

FLAVOR ______

FEEL ______

OVERALL ______

WHAT WORKED?

______

WHAT DIDN'T?

______

NAME ____ TYPE ____
PROPERTIES I'M GOING FOR ____
____
FORM ____
NOTES ____
____
FLAVOR/AROMA/PROCESS ____

Ingredients

Yeast

NAME ____
MANUFACTURER ____
LAST CULTURED ____

Water

pH TREATMENT ○ YES ○ NO
TYPE ____

Grain

NAME ____
ORIGIN ____
TYPE ____
ROASTED/TOASTED ____

○ WHEAT ____% ○ CORN ____%
○ BARLEY ____% ○ OATS ____%
○ MALT ____% ○ RICE ____%
○ RYE ____% ○ OTHER ____%

SPECIFIC PROPERTIES ____

Hops

VARIETY ____
SPECIFIC PROPERTIES ____
____
____
% AMOUNT ____
ORIGIN/NAME ____

Sugar

GRANULATED SUGAR ____
BROWN SUGAR ____
HONEY ____
MAPLE SYRUP ____
CORN SYRUP ____
MALT ____
MOLASSES ____
OTHER ____

Other Flavorings

TYPE ____
AMOUNT ____
USED FOR ____
ADDED DURING ____

NOTES ____
____
____
____
____
____
____

Brewing Log

DATE BREWED ______

BATCH SIZE ______

TASTING NOTES ______

______

______

BEGINNING SPECIFIC GRAVITY ______

FINAL SPECIFIC GRAVITY ______

______ % ALCOHOL ______

Boil + Mash

TEMPERATURE OF GRAIN ______

TEMPERATURE OF TUN ______

BOIL TIME ______

COOLING TIME & TEMPERATURE ______

Hops added

BOIL TIME ______

COOLING TIME & TEMPERATURE ______

SPECIFIC GRAVITY ______

Yeast added

TEMPERATURE ______

LENGTH OF FERMENT ______

BOTTLING GRAVITY ______

TYPE OF VESSEL ______

PRIMER & AMOUNT ______

Storing and Aging

AGED FOR ______

STORAGE TEMPERATURE ______

NOTES ______

Tasting and Visual Notes

______ OG ______ SRM

______ ABV ______ IBUs

APPEARANCE ______

AROMA ______

FLAVOR ______

FEEL ______

OVERALL ______

WHAT WORKED?

______

______

______

WHAT DIDN'T?

______

______

______

NAME ______ TYPE ______
PROPERTIES I'M GOING FOR ______
FORM ______
NOTES ______
FLAVOR/AROMA/PROCESS ______

Ingredients

Yeast

NAME ______
MANUFACTURER ______
LAST CULTURED ______

Water

pH TREATMENT ○ YES ○ NO
TYPE ______

Grain

NAME ______
ORIGIN ______
TYPE ______
ROASTED/TOASTED ______

○ WHEAT ____% ○ CORN ____%
○ BARLEY ____% ○ OATS ____%
○ MALT ____% ○ RICE ____%
○ RYE ____% ○ OTHER ____%

SPECIFIC PROPERTIES ______

Hops

VARIETY ______
SPECIFIC PROPERTIES ______
% AMOUNT ______
ORIGIN/NAME ______

Sugar

GRANULATED SUGAR ______
BROWN SUGAR ______
HONEY ______
MAPLE SYRUP ______
CORN SYRUP ______
MALT ______
MOLASSES ______
OTHER ______

Other Flavorings

TYPE ______
AMOUNT ______
USED FOR ______
ADDED DURING ______

NOTES ______

Brewing Log

DATE BREWED ____________________

BATCH SIZE ____________________

TASTING NOTES ____________________

BEGINNING SPECIFIC GRAVITY ________

FINAL SPECIFIC GRAVITY ________

____ % ALCOHOL ________

Boil + Mash

TEMPERATURE OF GRAIN ____________

TEMPERATURE OF TUN ____________

BOIL TIME ____________

COOLING TIME & TEMPERATURE ____________

Hops added

BOIL TIME ____________

COOLING TIME & TEMPERATURE ____________

SPECIFIC GRAVITY ____________

Yeast added

TEMPERATURE ____________

LENGTH OF FERMENT ____________

BOTTLING GRAVITY ____________

TYPE OF VESSEL ____________

PRIMER & AMOUNT ____________

Storing and Aging

AGED FOR ____________

STORAGE TEMPERATURE ____________

NOTES ____________________

Tasting and Visual Notes

____ OG ____ SRM

____ ABV ____ IBUs

APPEARANCE ____________________

AROMA ____________________

FLAVOR ____________________

FEEL ____________________

OVERALL ____________________

WHAT WORKED?

WHAT DIDN'T?

NAME TYPE
PROPERTIES I'M GOING FOR
FORM
NOTES
FLAVOR/AROMA/PROCESS

Ingredients

Yeast

NAME

MANUFACTURER

LAST CULTURED

Grain

NAME

ORIGIN

TYPE

ROASTED/TOASTED

- WHEAT ___%
- BARLEY ___%
- MALT ___%
- RYE ___%
- CORN ___%
- OATS ___%
- RICE ___%
- OTHER ___%

SPECIFIC PROPERTIES

Sugar

GRANULATED SUGAR

BROWN SUGAR

HONEY

MAPLE SYRUP

CORN SYRUP

MALT

MOLASSES

OTHER

Water

pH TREATMENT YES NO

TYPE

Hops

VARIETY

SPECIFIC PROPERTIES

% AMOUNT

ORIGIN/NAME

Other Flavorings

TYPE

AMOUNT

USED FOR

ADDED DURING

NOTES

Brewing Log

DATE BREWED ______

BATCH SIZE ______

TASTING NOTES ______

______

______

BEGINNING SPECIFIC GRAVITY ______

FINAL SPECIFIC GRAVITY ______

______ % ALCOHOL ______

Boil + Mash

TEMPERATURE OF GRAIN ______

TEMPERATURE OF TUN ______

BOIL TIME ______

COOLING TIME & TEMPERATURE ______

Hops added

BOIL TIME ______

COOLING TIME & TEMPERATURE ______

SPECIFIC GRAVITY ______

Yeast added

TEMPERATURE ______

LENGTH OF FERMENT ______

BOTTLING GRAVITY ______

TYPE OF VESSEL ______

PRIMER & AMOUNT ______

Storing and Aging

AGED FOR ______

STORAGE TEMPERATURE ______

NOTES ______

Tasting and Visual Notes

______ OG ______ SRM

______ ABV ______ IBUs

APPEARANCE ______

AROMA ______

FLAVOR ______

FEEL ______

OVERALL ______

WHAT WORKED?

______

WHAT DIDN'T?

______

NAME ______ TYPE ______
PROPERTIES I'M GOING FOR ______
FORM ______
NOTES ______
FLAVOR/AROMA/PROCESS ______

Ingredients

Yeast

NAME ______
MANUFACTURER ______
LAST CULTURED ______

Water

pH TREATMENT ○ YES ○ NO
TYPE ______

Grain

NAME ______
ORIGIN ______
TYPE ______
ROASTED/TOASTED ______

○ WHEAT ____% ○ CORN ____%
○ BARLEY ____% ○ OATS ____%
○ MALT ____% ○ RICE ____%
○ RYE ____% ○ OTHER ____%

SPECIFIC PROPERTIES ______

Hops

VARIETY ______
SPECIFIC PROPERTIES ______
% AMOUNT ______
ORIGIN/NAME ______

Sugar

GRANULATED SUGAR ______
BROWN SUGAR ______
HONEY ______
MAPLE SYRUP ______
CORN SYRUP ______
MALT ______
MOLASSES ______
OTHER ______

Other Flavorings

TYPE ______
AMOUNT ______
USED FOR ______
ADDED DURING ______

NOTES ______

Brewing Log

DATE BREWED ______

BATCH SIZE ______

TASTING NOTES ______

______

______

BEGINNING SPECIFIC GRAVITY ______

FINAL SPECIFIC GRAVITY ______

______ % ALCOHOL ______

Boil + Mash

TEMPERATURE OF GRAIN ______

TEMPERATURE OF TUN ______

BOIL TIME ______

COOLING TIME & TEMPERATURE ______

Hops added

BOIL TIME ______

COOLING TIME & TEMPERATURE ______

SPECIFIC GRAVITY ______

Yeast added

TEMPERATURE ______

LENGTH OF FERMENT ______

BOTTLING GRAVITY ______

TYPE OF VESSEL ______

PRIMER & AMOUNT ______

Storing and Aging

AGED FOR ______

STORAGE TEMPERATURE ______

NOTES ______

Tasting and Visual Notes

______ OG ______ SRM

______ ABV ______ IBUs

APPEARANCE ______

AROMA ______

FLAVOR ______

FEEL ______

OVERALL ______

WHAT WORKED?

______

WHAT DIDN'T?

______

NAME TYPE
PROPERTIES I'M GOING FOR
FORM
NOTES
FLAVOR/AROMA/PROCESS

Ingredients

Yeast

NAME
MANUFACTURER
LAST CULTURED

Grain

NAME
ORIGIN
TYPE
ROASTED/TOASTED

- WHEAT ___%
- BARLEY ___%
- MALT ___%
- RYE ___%
- CORN ___%
- OATS ___%
- RICE ___%
- OTHER ___%

SPECIFIC PROPERTIES

Sugar

GRANULATED SUGAR
BROWN SUGAR
HONEY
MAPLE SYRUP
CORN SYRUP
MALT
MOLASSES
OTHER

Water

pH TREATMENT ◯ YES ◯ NO
TYPE

Hops

VARIETY
SPECIFIC PROPERTIES
% AMOUNT
ORIGIN/NAME

Other Flavorings

TYPE
AMOUNT
USED FOR
ADDED DURING

NOTES

Brewing Log

DATE BREWED ______________________

BATCH SIZE ______________________

TASTING NOTES ______________________

____

____

BEGINNING SPECIFIC GRAVITY ______

FINAL SPECIFIC GRAVITY ______

______ % ALCOHOL ______

Boil + Mash

TEMPERATURE OF GRAIN ______________________

TEMPERATURE OF TUN ______________________

BOIL TIME ______________________

COOLING TIME & TEMPERATURE ______________________

Hops added

BOIL TIME ______________________

COOLING TIME & TEMPERATURE ______________________

SPECIFIC GRAVITY ______________________

Yeast added

TEMPERATURE ______________________

LENGTH OF FERMENT ______________________

BOTTLING GRAVITY ______________________

TYPE OF VESSEL ______________________

PRIMER & AMOUNT ______________________

Storing and Aging

AGED FOR ______________________

STORAGE TEMPERATURE ______________________

NOTES ______________________

Tasting and Visual Notes

______ OG ______ SRM

______ ABV ______ IBUs

APPEARANCE ______________________

AROMA ______________________

FLAVOR ______________________

FEEL ______________________

OVERALL ______________________

WHAT WORKED?

____

____

____

WHAT DIDN'T?

____

____

____

NAME ____ TYPE ____
PROPERTIES I'M GOING FOR ____
____
FORM ____
NOTES ____
____
FLAVOR/AROMA/PROCESS ____

Ingredients

Yeast

NAME ____
MANUFACTURER ____
LAST CULTURED ____

Water

pH TREATMENT ○ YES ○ NO
TYPE ____

Grain

NAME ____
ORIGIN ____
TYPE ____
ROASTED/TOASTED ____

○ WHEAT ____%
○ BARLEY ____%
○ MALT ____%
○ RYE ____%
○ CORN ____%
○ OATS ____%
○ RICE ____%
○ OTHER ____%

SPECIFIC PROPERTIES ____

Hops

VARIETY ____
SPECIFIC PROPERTIES ____
____
____
% AMOUNT ____
ORIGIN/NAME ____

Sugar

GRANULATED SUGAR ____
BROWN SUGAR ____
HONEY ____
MAPLE SYRUP ____
CORN SYRUP ____
MALT ____
MOLASSES ____
OTHER ____

Other Flavorings

TYPE ____
AMOUNT ____
USED FOR ____
ADDED DURING ____

NOTES ____
____
____
____
____
____
____

Brewing Log

DATE BREWED __________

BATCH SIZE __________

TASTING NOTES __________

BEGINNING SPECIFIC GRAVITY __________

FINAL SPECIFIC GRAVITY __________

_____ % ALCOHOL __________

Boil + Mash

TEMPERATURE OF GRAIN __________

TEMPERATURE OF TUN __________

BOIL TIME __________

COOLING TIME & TEMPERATURE __________

Hops added

BOIL TIME __________

COOLING TIME & TEMPERATURE __________

SPECIFIC GRAVITY __________

Yeast added

TEMPERATURE __________

LENGTH OF FERMENT __________

BOTTLING GRAVITY __________

TYPE OF VESSEL __________

PRIMER & AMOUNT __________

Storing and Aging

AGED FOR __________

STORAGE TEMPERATURE __________

NOTES __________

Tasting and Visual Notes

_____ OG _____ SRM

_____ ABV _____ IBUs

APPEARANCE __________

AROMA __________

FLAVOR __________

FEEL __________

OVERALL __________

WHAT WORKED?

WHAT DIDN'T?

NAME | TYPE
PROPERTIES I'M GOING FOR
FORM
NOTES
FLAVOR/AROMA/PROCESS

Ingredients

Yeast

NAME

MANUFACTURER

LAST CULTURED

Water

pH TREATMENT ○ YES ○ NO

TYPE

Grain

NAME

ORIGIN

TYPE

ROASTED/TOASTED

○ WHEAT ___%
○ BARLEY ___%
○ MALT ___%
○ RYE ___%
○ CORN ___%
○ OATS ___%
○ RICE ___%
○ OTHER ___%

SPECIFIC PROPERTIES

Hops

VARIETY

SPECIFIC PROPERTIES

% AMOUNT

ORIGIN/NAME

Sugar

GRANULATED SUGAR

BROWN SUGAR

HONEY

MAPLE SYRUP

CORN SYRUP

MALT

MOLASSES

OTHER

Other Flavorings

TYPE

AMOUNT

USED FOR

ADDED DURING

NOTES

Brewing Log

DATE BREWED ______________________

BATCH SIZE ______________________

TASTING NOTES ______________________

____

____

BEGINNING SPECIFIC GRAVITY __________

FINAL SPECIFIC GRAVITY __________

______ % ALCOHOL __________

Boil + Mash

TEMPERATURE OF GRAIN __________

TEMPERATURE OF TUN __________

BOIL TIME __________

COOLING TIME & TEMPERATURE __________

Hops added

BOIL TIME __________

COOLING TIME & TEMPERATURE __________

SPECIFIC GRAVITY __________

Yeast added

TEMPERATURE __________

LENGTH OF FERMENT __________

BOTTLING GRAVITY __________

TYPE OF VESSEL __________

PRIMER & AMOUNT __________

Storing and Aging

AGED FOR __________

STORAGE TEMPERATURE __________

NOTES __________

Tasting and Visual Notes

______ OG ______ SRM

______ ABV ______ IBUs

APPEARANCE __________

AROMA __________

FLAVOR __________

FEEL __________

OVERALL __________

WHAT WORKED?

____

____

____

WHAT DIDN'T?

____

____

____

NAME
TYPE
PROPERTIES I'M GOING FOR
FORM
NOTES
FLAVOR/AROMA/PROCESS

Ingredients

Yeast

NAME

MANUFACTURER

LAST CULTURED

Water

pH TREATMENT ○ YES ○ NO

TYPE

Grain

NAME

ORIGIN

TYPE

ROASTED/TOASTED

○ WHEAT ___%
○ BARLEY ___%
○ MALT ___%
○ RYE ___%
○ CORN ___%
○ OATS ___%
○ RICE ___%
○ OTHER ___%

SPECIFIC PROPERTIES

Hops

VARIETY

SPECIFIC PROPERTIES

% AMOUNT

ORIGIN/NAME

Sugar

GRANULATED SUGAR

BROWN SUGAR

HONEY

MAPLE SYRUP

CORN SYRUP

MALT

MOLASSES

OTHER

Other Flavorings

TYPE

AMOUNT

USED FOR

ADDED DURING

NOTES

Brewing Log

DATE BREWED ______________________

BATCH SIZE ______________________

TASTING NOTES ______________________

____

____

BEGINNING SPECIFIC GRAVITY __________

FINAL SPECIFIC GRAVITY __________

______ % ALCOHOL __________

Boil + Mash

TEMPERATURE OF GRAIN ______________

TEMPERATURE OF TUN ______________

BOIL TIME ______________

COOLING TIME & TEMPERATURE ______________

Hops added

BOIL TIME ______________

COOLING TIME & TEMPERATURE ______________

SPECIFIC GRAVITY ______________

Yeast added

TEMPERATURE ______________

LENGTH OF FERMENT ______________

BOTTLING GRAVITY ______________

TYPE OF VESSEL ______________

PRIMER & AMOUNT ______________

Storing and Aging

AGED FOR ______________

STORAGE TEMPERATURE ______________

NOTES ______________________

Tasting and Visual Notes

______ OG ______ SRM

______ ABV ______ IBUs

APPEARANCE ______________________

AROMA ______________________

FLAVOR ______________________

FEEL ______________________

OVERALL ______________________

WHAT WORKED?

____

____

____

WHAT DIDN'T?

____

____

____

NAME ____ TYPE ____
PROPERTIES I'M GOING FOR ____
FORM ____
NOTES ____
FLAVOR/AROMA/PROCESS ____

Ingredients

Yeast
NAME ____
MANUFACTURER ____
LAST CULTURED ____

Water
pH TREATMENT ○ YES ○ NO
TYPE ____

Grain
NAME ____
ORIGIN ____
TYPE ____
ROASTED/TOASTED ____

○ WHEAT ____% ○ CORN ____%
○ BARLEY ____% ○ OATS ____%
○ MALT ____% ○ RICE ____%
○ RYE ____% ○ OTHER ____%

SPECIFIC PROPERTIES ____

Hops
VARIETY ____
SPECIFIC PROPERTIES ____
% AMOUNT ____
ORIGIN/NAME ____

Sugar
GRANULATED SUGAR ____
BROWN SUGAR ____
HONEY ____
MAPLE SYRUP ____
CORN SYRUP ____
MALT ____
MOLASSES ____
OTHER ____

Other Flavorings
TYPE ____
AMOUNT ____
USED FOR ____
ADDED DURING ____

NOTES ____

Brewing Log

DATE BREWED ______
BATCH SIZE ______
TASTING NOTES ______

BEGINNING SPECIFIC GRAVITY ______
FINAL SPECIFIC GRAVITY ______
______ % ALCOHOL ______

Boil + Mash

TEMPERATURE OF GRAIN ______
TEMPERATURE OF TUN ______
BOIL TIME ______
COOLING TIME & TEMPERATURE ______

Hops added

BOIL TIME ______
COOLING TIME & TEMPERATURE ______
SPECIFIC GRAVITY ______

Yeast added

TEMPERATURE ______
LENGTH OF FERMENT ______
BOTTLING GRAVITY ______
TYPE OF VESSEL ______
PRIMER & AMOUNT ______

Storing and Aging

AGED FOR ______
STORAGE TEMPERATURE ______

NOTES ______

Tasting and Visual Notes

______ OG ______ SRM
______ ABV ______ IBUs

APPEARANCE ______
AROMA ______
FLAVOR ______
FEEL ______
OVERALL ______

WHAT WORKED?

WHAT DIDN'T?

NAME TYPE
PROPERTIES I'M GOING FOR
FORM
NOTES
FLAVOR/AROMA/PROCESS

Ingredients

Yeast

NAME
MANUFACTURER
LAST CULTURED

Water

pH TREATMENT ○ YES ○ NO
TYPE

Grain

NAME
ORIGIN
TYPE
ROASTED/TOASTED

○ WHEAT ____%
○ BARLEY ____%
○ MALT ____%
○ RYE ____%
○ CORN ____%
○ OATS ____%
○ RICE ____%
○ OTHER ____%

SPECIFIC PROPERTIES

Hops

VARIETY
SPECIFIC PROPERTIES
% AMOUNT
ORIGIN/NAME

Sugar

GRANULATED SUGAR
BROWN SUGAR
HONEY
MAPLE SYRUP
CORN SYRUP
MALT
MOLASSES
OTHER

Other Flavorings

TYPE
AMOUNT
USED FOR
ADDED DURING

NOTES

Brewing Log

DATE BREWED ______________________

BATCH SIZE ______________________

TASTING NOTES ______________________

____

____

BEGINNING SPECIFIC GRAVITY __________

FINAL SPECIFIC GRAVITY __________

______ % ALCOHOL __________

Boil + Mash

TEMPERATURE OF GRAIN ______________________

TEMPERATURE OF TUN ______________________

BOIL TIME ______________________

COOLING TIME & TEMPERATURE ______________________

Hops added

BOIL TIME ______________________

COOLING TIME & TEMPERATURE ______________________

SPECIFIC GRAVITY ______________________

Yeast added

TEMPERATURE ______________________

LENGTH OF FERMENT ______________________

BOTTLING GRAVITY ______________________

TYPE OF VESSEL ______________________

PRIMER & AMOUNT ______________________

Storing and Aging

AGED FOR ______________________

STORAGE TEMPERATURE ______________________

NOTES ______________________

Tasting and Visual Notes

______ OG ______ SRM

______ ABV ______ IBUs

APPEARANCE ______________________

AROMA ______________________

FLAVOR ______________________

FEEL ______________________

OVERALL ______________________

WHAT WORKED?

____

____

____

WHAT DIDN'T?

____

____

____

NAME ______ TYPE ______

PROPERTIES I'M GOING FOR ______

FORM ______

NOTES ______

FLAVOR/AROMA/PROCESS ______

Ingredients

Yeast

NAME ______

MANUFACTURER ______

LAST CULTURED ______

Water

pH TREATMENT ○ YES ○ NO

TYPE ______

Grain

NAME ______

ORIGIN ______

TYPE ______

ROASTED/TOASTED ______

○ WHEAT ____% ○ CORN ____%

○ BARLEY ____% ○ OATS ____%

○ MALT ____% ○ RICE ____%

○ RYE ____% ○ OTHER ____%

SPECIFIC PROPERTIES ______

Hops

VARIETY ______

SPECIFIC PROPERTIES ______

% AMOUNT ______

ORIGIN/NAME ______

Sugar

GRANULATED SUGAR ______

BROWN SUGAR ______

HONEY ______

MAPLE SYRUP ______

CORN SYRUP ______

MALT ______

MOLASSES ______

OTHER ______

Other Flavorings

TYPE ______

AMOUNT ______

USED FOR ______

ADDED DURING ______

NOTES ______

Brewing Log

DATE BREWED ______

BATCH SIZE ______

TASTING NOTES ______

BEGINNING SPECIFIC GRAVITY ______

FINAL SPECIFIC GRAVITY ______

______ % ALCOHOL ______

Boil + Mash

TEMPERATURE OF GRAIN ______

TEMPERATURE OF TUN ______

BOIL TIME ______

COOLING TIME & TEMPERATURE ______

Hops added

BOIL TIME ______

COOLING TIME & TEMPERATURE ______

SPECIFIC GRAVITY ______

Yeast added

TEMPERATURE ______

LENGTH OF FERMENT ______

BOTTLING GRAVITY ______

TYPE OF VESSEL ______

PRIMER & AMOUNT ______

Storing and Aging

AGED FOR ______

STORAGE TEMPERATURE ______

NOTES ______

Tasting and Visual Notes

______ OG ______ SRM

______ ABV ______ IBUs

APPEARANCE ______

AROMA ______

FLAVOR ______

FEEL ______

OVERALL ______

WHAT WORKED?

WHAT DIDN'T?

NAME ______ TYPE ______

PROPERTIES I'M GOING FOR ______

FORM ______

NOTES ______

FLAVOR/AROMA/PROCESS ______

Ingredients

Yeast

NAME ______

MANUFACTURER ______

LAST CULTURED ______

Water

pH TREATMENT ○ YES ○ NO

TYPE ______

Grain

NAME ______

ORIGIN ______

TYPE ______

ROASTED/TOASTED ______

○ WHEAT ____%	○ CORN ____%
○ BARLEY ____%	○ OATS ____%
○ MALT ____%	○ RICE ____%
○ RYE ____%	○ OTHER ____%

SPECIFIC PROPERTIES ______

Hops

VARIETY ______

SPECIFIC PROPERTIES ______

% AMOUNT ______

ORIGIN/NAME ______

Sugar

GRANULATED SUGAR ______

BROWN SUGAR ______

HONEY ______

MAPLE SYRUP ______

CORN SYRUP ______

MALT ______

MOLASSES ______

OTHER ______

Other Flavorings

TYPE ______

AMOUNT ______

USED FOR ______

ADDED DURING ______

NOTES ______

Brewing Log

DATE BREWED ______
BATCH SIZE ______
TASTING NOTES ______

BEGINNING SPECIFIC GRAVITY ______
FINAL SPECIFIC GRAVITY ______
______ % ALCOHOL ______

Boil + Mash

TEMPERATURE OF GRAIN ______
TEMPERATURE OF TUN ______
BOIL TIME ______
COOLING TIME & TEMPERATURE ______

Hops added

BOIL TIME ______
COOLING TIME & TEMPERATURE ______
SPECIFIC GRAVITY ______

Yeast added

TEMPERATURE ______
LENGTH OF FERMENT ______
BOTTLING GRAVITY ______
TYPE OF VESSEL ______
PRIMER & AMOUNT ______

Storing and Aging

AGED FOR ______
STORAGE TEMPERATURE ______

NOTES ______

Tasting and Visual Notes

______ OG ______ SRM
______ ABV ______ IBUs

APPEARANCE ______
AROMA ______
FLAVOR ______
FEEL ______
OVERALL ______

WHAT WORKED?

WHAT DIDN'T?

NAME ______ TYPE ______

PROPERTIES I'M GOING FOR ______

FORM ______

NOTES ______

FLAVOR/AROMA/PROCESS ______

Ingredients

Yeast

NAME ______

MANUFACTURER ______

LAST CULTURED ______

Water

pH TREATMENT ○ YES ○ NO

TYPE ______

Grain

NAME ______

ORIGIN ______

TYPE ______

ROASTED/TOASTED ______

○ WHEAT ______%
○ CORN ______%
○ BARLEY ______%
○ OATS ______%
○ MALT ______%
○ RICE ______%
○ RYE ______%
○ OTHER ______%

SPECIFIC PROPERTIES ______

Hops

VARIETY ______

SPECIFIC PROPERTIES ______

% AMOUNT ______

ORIGIN/NAME ______

Sugar

GRANULATED SUGAR ______

BROWN SUGAR ______

HONEY ______

MAPLE SYRUP ______

CORN SYRUP ______

MALT ______

MOLASSES ______

OTHER ______

Other Flavorings

TYPE ______

AMOUNT ______

USED FOR ______

ADDED DURING ______

NOTES ______

Brewing Log

DATE BREWED

BATCH SIZE

TASTING NOTES

BEGINNING SPECIFIC GRAVITY

FINAL SPECIFIC GRAVITY

% ALCOHOL

Boil + Mash

TEMPERATURE OF GRAIN

TEMPERATURE OF TUN

BOIL TIME

COOLING TIME & TEMPERATURE

Hops added

BOIL TIME

COOLING TIME & TEMPERATURE

SPECIFIC GRAVITY

Yeast added

TEMPERATURE

LENGTH OF FERMENT

BOTTLING GRAVITY

TYPE OF VESSEL

PRIMER & AMOUNT

Storing and Aging

AGED FOR

STORAGE TEMPERATURE

NOTES

Tasting and Visual Notes

OG

SRM

ABV

IBUs

APPEARANCE

AROMA

FLAVOR

FEEL

OVERALL

WHAT WORKED?

WHAT DIDN'T?

NAME TYPE

PROPERTIES I'M GOING FOR

FORM

NOTES

FLAVOR/AROMA/PROCESS

Ingredients

Yeast

NAME

MANUFACTURER

LAST CULTURED

Water

pH TREATMENT ○ YES ○ NO

TYPE

Grain

NAME

ORIGIN

TYPE

ROASTED/TOASTED

○ WHEAT ____% ○ CORN ____%

○ BARLEY ____% ○ OATS ____%

○ MALT ____% ○ RICE ____%

○ RYE ____% ○ OTHER ____%

SPECIFIC PROPERTIES

Hops

VARIETY

SPECIFIC PROPERTIES

% AMOUNT

ORIGIN/NAME

Sugar

GRANULATED SUGAR

BROWN SUGAR

HONEY

MAPLE SYRUP

CORN SYRUP

MALT

MOLASSES

OTHER

Other Flavorings

TYPE

AMOUNT

USED FOR

ADDED DURING

NOTES

Brewing Log

DATE BREWED

BATCH SIZE

TASTING NOTES

BEGINNING SPECIFIC GRAVITY

FINAL SPECIFIC GRAVITY

% ALCOHOL

Boil + Mash

TEMPERATURE OF GRAIN

TEMPERATURE OF TUN

BOIL TIME

COOLING TIME & TEMPERATURE

Hops added

BOIL TIME

COOLING TIME & TEMPERATURE

SPECIFIC GRAVITY

Yeast added

TEMPERATURE

LENGTH OF FERMENT

BOTTLING GRAVITY

TYPE OF VESSEL

PRIMER & AMOUNT

Storing and Aging

AGED FOR

STORAGE TEMPERATURE

NOTES

Tasting and Visual Notes

OG

SRM

ABV

IBUs

APPEARANCE

AROMA

FLAVOR

FEEL

OVERALL

WHAT WORKED?

WHAT DIDN'T?

NAME | TYPE
PROPERTIES I'M GOING FOR
FORM
NOTES
FLAVOR/AROMA/PROCESS

Ingredients

Yeast

NAME
MANUFACTURER
LAST CULTURED

Water

pH TREATMENT ○ YES ○ NO
TYPE

Grain

NAME
ORIGIN
TYPE
ROASTED/TOASTED

○ WHEAT	____%	○ CORN	____%
○ BARLEY	____%	○ OATS	____%
○ MALT	____%	○ RICE	____%
○ RYE	____%	○ OTHER	____%

SPECIFIC PROPERTIES

Hops

VARIETY
SPECIFIC PROPERTIES
% AMOUNT
ORIGIN/NAME

Sugar

GRANULATED SUGAR
BROWN SUGAR
HONEY
MAPLE SYRUP
CORN SYRUP
MALT
MOLASSES
OTHER

Other Flavorings

TYPE
AMOUNT
USED FOR
ADDED DURING

NOTES

Brewing Log

DATE BREWED ______

BATCH SIZE ______

TASTING NOTES ______

BEGINNING SPECIFIC GRAVITY ______

FINAL SPECIFIC GRAVITY ______

______ % ALCOHOL ______

Boil + Mash

TEMPERATURE OF GRAIN ______

TEMPERATURE OF TUN ______

BOIL TIME ______

COOLING TIME & TEMPERATURE ______

Hops added

BOIL TIME ______

COOLING TIME & TEMPERATURE ______

SPECIFIC GRAVITY ______

Yeast added

TEMPERATURE ______

LENGTH OF FERMENT ______

BOTTLING GRAVITY ______

TYPE OF VESSEL ______

PRIMER & AMOUNT ______

Storing and Aging

AGED FOR ______

STORAGE TEMPERATURE ______

NOTES ______

Tasting and Visual Notes

______ OG ______ SRM

______ ABV ______ IBUs

APPEARANCE ______

AROMA ______

FLAVOR ______

FEEL ______

OVERALL ______

WHAT WORKED?

WHAT DIDN'T?

NAME ____ TYPE ____
PROPERTIES I'M GOING FOR ____
FORM ____
NOTES ____
FLAVOR/AROMA/PROCESS ____

Ingredients

Yeast

NAME ____
MANUFACTURER ____
LAST CULTURED ____

Water

pH TREATMENT ○ YES ○ NO
TYPE ____

Grain

NAME ____
ORIGIN ____
TYPE ____
ROASTED/TOASTED ____

○ WHEAT ____%   ○ CORN ____%
○ BARLEY ____%   ○ OATS ____%
○ MALT ____%   ○ RICE ____%
○ RYE ____%   ○ OTHER ____%

SPECIFIC PROPERTIES ____

Hops

VARIETY ____
SPECIFIC PROPERTIES ____
% AMOUNT ____
ORIGIN/NAME ____

Sugar

GRANULATED SUGAR ____
BROWN SUGAR ____
HONEY ____
MAPLE SYRUP ____
CORN SYRUP ____
MALT ____
MOLASSES ____
OTHER ____

Other Flavorings

TYPE ____
AMOUNT ____
USED FOR ____
ADDED DURING ____

NOTES ____

Brewing Log

DATE BREWED ______

BATCH SIZE ______

TASTING NOTES ______

BEGINNING SPECIFIC GRAVITY ______

FINAL SPECIFIC GRAVITY ______

______ % ALCOHOL ______

Boil + Mash

TEMPERATURE OF GRAIN ______

TEMPERATURE OF TUN ______

BOIL TIME ______

COOLING TIME & TEMPERATURE ______

Hops added

BOIL TIME ______

COOLING TIME & TEMPERATURE ______

SPECIFIC GRAVITY ______

Yeast added

TEMPERATURE ______

LENGTH OF FERMENT ______

BOTTLING GRAVITY ______

TYPE OF VESSEL ______

PRIMER & AMOUNT ______

Storing and Aging

AGED FOR ______

STORAGE TEMPERATURE ______

NOTES ______

Tasting and Visual Notes

______ OG ______ SRM

______ ABV ______ IBUs

APPEARANCE ______

AROMA ______

FLAVOR ______

FEEL ______

OVERALL ______

WHAT WORKED?

WHAT DIDN'T?

NAME | TYPE
PROPERTIES I'M GOING FOR
FORM
NOTES
FLAVOR/AROMA/PROCESS

Ingredients

Yeast

NAME
MANUFACTURER
LAST CULTURED

Water

pH TREATMENT ○ YES ○ NO
TYPE

Grain

NAME
ORIGIN
TYPE
ROASTED/TOASTED

○ WHEAT ____%
○ BARLEY ____%
○ MALT ____%
○ RYE ____%
○ CORN ____%
○ OATS ____%
○ RICE ____%
○ OTHER ____%

SPECIFIC PROPERTIES

Hops

VARIETY
SPECIFIC PROPERTIES
% AMOUNT
ORIGIN/NAME

Sugar

GRANULATED SUGAR
BROWN SUGAR
HONEY
MAPLE SYRUP
CORN SYRUP
MALT
MOLASSES
OTHER

Other Flavorings

TYPE
AMOUNT
USED FOR
ADDED DURING

NOTES

Brewing Log

DATE BREWED ______

BATCH SIZE ______

TASTING NOTES ______

______

______

BEGINNING SPECIFIC GRAVITY ______

FINAL SPECIFIC GRAVITY ______

______ % ALCOHOL ______

Boil + Mash

TEMPERATURE OF GRAIN ______

TEMPERATURE OF TUN ______

BOIL TIME ______

COOLING TIME & TEMPERATURE ______

Hops added

BOIL TIME ______

COOLING TIME & TEMPERATURE ______

SPECIFIC GRAVITY ______

Yeast added

TEMPERATURE ______

LENGTH OF FERMENT ______

BOTTLING GRAVITY ______

TYPE OF VESSEL ______

PRIMER & AMOUNT ______

Storing and Aging

AGED FOR ______

STORAGE TEMPERATURE ______

NOTES ______

Tasting and Visual Notes

______ OG ______ SRM

______ ABV ______ IBUs

APPEARANCE ______

AROMA ______

FLAVOR ______

FEEL ______

OVERALL ______

WHAT WORKED?

______

WHAT DIDN'T?

______

NAME | TYPE
PROPERTIES I'M GOING FOR
FORM
NOTES
FLAVOR/AROMA/PROCESS

Ingredients

Yeast

NAME ____
MANUFACTURER ____
LAST CULTURED ____

Water

pH TREATMENT ○ YES ○ NO
TYPE ____

Grain

NAME ____
ORIGIN ____
TYPE ____
ROASTED/TOASTED ____

○ WHEAT ____% ○ CORN ____%
○ BARLEY ____% ○ OATS ____%
○ MALT ____% ○ RICE ____%
○ RYE ____% ○ OTHER ____%

SPECIFIC PROPERTIES ____

Hops

VARIETY ____
SPECIFIC PROPERTIES ____
% AMOUNT ____
ORIGIN/NAME ____

Sugar

GRANULATED SUGAR ____
BROWN SUGAR ____
HONEY ____
MAPLE SYRUP ____
CORN SYRUP ____
MALT ____
MOLASSES ____
OTHER ____

Other Flavorings

TYPE ____
AMOUNT ____
USED FOR ____
ADDED DURING ____

NOTES ____

Brewing Log

DATE BREWED ______
BATCH SIZE ______
TASTING NOTES ______

BEGINNING SPECIFIC GRAVITY ______
FINAL SPECIFIC GRAVITY ______
______ % ALCOHOL ______

Boil + Mash

TEMPERATURE OF GRAIN ______
TEMPERATURE OF TUN ______
BOIL TIME ______
COOLING TIME & TEMPERATURE ______

Hops added

BOIL TIME ______
COOLING TIME & TEMPERATURE ______
SPECIFIC GRAVITY ______

Yeast added

TEMPERATURE ______
LENGTH OF FERMENT ______
BOTTLING GRAVITY ______
TYPE OF VESSEL ______
PRIMER & AMOUNT ______

Storing and Aging

AGED FOR ______
STORAGE TEMPERATURE ______

NOTES ______

Tasting and Visual Notes

______ OG ______ SRM
______ ABV ______ IBUs

APPEARANCE ______
AROMA ______
FLAVOR ______
FEEL ______
OVERALL ______

WHAT WORKED?

WHAT DIDN'T?

NAME ______ TYPE ______

PROPERTIES I'M GOING FOR ______

FORM ______

NOTES ______

FLAVOR/AROMA/PROCESS ______

Ingredients

Yeast

NAME ______

MANUFACTURER ______

LAST CULTURED ______

Water

pH TREATMENT ○ YES ○ NO

TYPE ______

Grain

NAME ______

ORIGIN ______

TYPE ______

ROASTED/TOASTED ______

○ WHEAT ____% ○ CORN ____%

○ BARLEY ____% ○ OATS ____%

○ MALT ____% ○ RICE ____%

○ RYE ____% ○ OTHER ____%

SPECIFIC PROPERTIES ______

Hops

VARIETY ______

SPECIFIC PROPERTIES ______

% AMOUNT ______

ORIGIN/NAME ______

Sugar

GRANULATED SUGAR ______

BROWN SUGAR ______

HONEY ______

MAPLE SYRUP ______

CORN SYRUP ______

MALT ______

MOLASSES ______

OTHER ______

Other Flavorings

TYPE ______

AMOUNT ______

USED FOR ______

ADDED DURING ______

NOTES ______

Brewing Log

DATE BREWED ______

BATCH SIZE ______

TASTING NOTES ______

______

______

BEGINNING SPECIFIC GRAVITY ______

FINAL SPECIFIC GRAVITY ______

______ % ALCOHOL ______

Boil + Mash

TEMPERATURE OF GRAIN ______

TEMPERATURE OF TUN ______

BOIL TIME ______

COOLING TIME & TEMPERATURE ______

Hops added

BOIL TIME ______

COOLING TIME & TEMPERATURE ______

SPECIFIC GRAVITY ______

Yeast added

TEMPERATURE ______

LENGTH OF FERMENT ______

BOTTLING GRAVITY ______

TYPE OF VESSEL ______

PRIMER & AMOUNT ______

Storing and Aging

AGED FOR ______

STORAGE TEMPERATURE ______

NOTES ______

Tasting and Visual Notes

______ OG ______ SRM

______ ABV ______ IBUs

APPEARANCE ______

AROMA ______

FLAVOR ______

FEEL ______

OVERALL ______

WHAT WORKED?

______

WHAT DIDN'T?

______

NAME ____ TYPE ____
PROPERTIES I'M GOING FOR ____
____
FORM ____
NOTES ____
____
FLAVOR/AROMA/PROCESS ____

Ingredients

Yeast

NAME ____
MANUFACTURER ____
LAST CULTURED ____

Water

pH TREATMENT ◯ YES ◯ NO
TYPE ____

Grain

NAME ____
ORIGIN ____
TYPE ____
ROASTED/TOASTED ____

◯ WHEAT ____% ◯ CORN ____%
◯ BARLEY ____% ◯ OATS ____%
◯ MALT ____% ◯ RICE ____%
◯ RYE ____% ◯ OTHER ____%

SPECIFIC PROPERTIES ____

Hops

VARIETY ____
SPECIFIC PROPERTIES ____
____
____
% AMOUNT ____
ORIGIN/NAME ____

Sugar

GRANULATED SUGAR ____
BROWN SUGAR ____
HONEY ____
MAPLE SYRUP ____
CORN SYRUP ____
MALT ____
MOLASSES ____
OTHER ____

Other Flavorings

TYPE ____
AMOUNT ____
USED FOR ____
ADDED DURING ____

NOTES ____
____
____
____
____
____
____

Brewing Log

DATE BREWED ______________

BATCH SIZE ______________

TASTING NOTES ______________

____

____

BEGINNING SPECIFIC GRAVITY ______________

FINAL SPECIFIC GRAVITY ______________

______ % ALCOHOL ______________

Boil + Mash

TEMPERATURE OF GRAIN ______________

TEMPERATURE OF TUN ______________

BOIL TIME ______________

COOLING TIME & TEMPERATURE ______________

Hops added

BOIL TIME ______________

COOLING TIME & TEMPERATURE ______________

SPECIFIC GRAVITY ______________

Yeast added

TEMPERATURE ______________

LENGTH OF FERMENT ______________

BOTTLING GRAVITY ______________

TYPE OF VESSEL ______________

PRIMER & AMOUNT ______________

Storing and Aging

AGED FOR ______________

STORAGE TEMPERATURE ______________

NOTES ______________

Tasting and Visual Notes

______ OG ______ SRM

______ ABV ______ IBUs

APPEARANCE ______________

AROMA ______________

FLAVOR ______________

FEEL ______________

OVERALL ______________

WHAT WORKED?

____

____

____

WHAT DIDN'T?

____

____

____

NAME ____________ TYPE ____________

PROPERTIES I'M GOING FOR ____________

____

FORM ____________

NOTES ____________

____

FLAVOR/AROMA/PROCESS ____________

Ingredients

Yeast

NAME ____________

MANUFACTURER ____________

LAST CULTURED ____________

Water

pH TREATMENT ○ YES ○ NO

TYPE ____________

Grain

NAME ____________

ORIGIN ____________

TYPE ____________

ROASTED/TOASTED ____________

○ WHEAT ______% ○ CORN ______%

○ BARLEY ______% ○ OATS ______%

○ MALT ______% ○ RICE ______%

○ RYE ______% ○ OTHER ______%

SPECIFIC PROPERTIES ____________

Hops

VARIETY ____________

SPECIFIC PROPERTIES ____________

____

____

% AMOUNT ____________

ORIGIN/NAME ____________

Sugar

GRANULATED SUGAR ____________

BROWN SUGAR ____________

HONEY ____________

MAPLE SYRUP ____________

CORN SYRUP ____________

MALT ____________

MOLASSES ____________

OTHER ____________

Other Flavorings

TYPE ____________

AMOUNT ____________

USED FOR ____________

ADDED DURING ____________

NOTES ____________

____

____

____

____

____

____

Brewing Log

DATE BREWED ______

BATCH SIZE ______

TASTING NOTES ______

______

______

BEGINNING SPECIFIC GRAVITY ______

FINAL SPECIFIC GRAVITY ______

______ % ALCOHOL ______

Boil + Mash

TEMPERATURE OF GRAIN ______

TEMPERATURE OF TUN ______

BOIL TIME ______

COOLING TIME & TEMPERATURE ______

Hops added

BOIL TIME ______

COOLING TIME & TEMPERATURE ______

SPECIFIC GRAVITY ______

Yeast added

TEMPERATURE ______

LENGTH OF FERMENT ______

BOTTLING GRAVITY ______

TYPE OF VESSEL ______

PRIMER & AMOUNT ______

Storing and Aging

AGED FOR ______

STORAGE TEMPERATURE ______

NOTES ______

Tasting and Visual Notes

______ OG ______ SRM

______ ABV ______ IBUs

APPEARANCE ______

AROMA ______

FLAVOR ______

FEEL ______

OVERALL ______

WHAT WORKED?

______

WHAT DIDN'T?

______

NAME TYPE

PROPERTIES I'M GOING FOR

FORM

NOTES

FLAVOR/AROMA/PROCESS

Ingredients

Yeast

NAME

MANUFACTURER

LAST CULTURED

Water

pH TREATMENT ○ YES ○ NO

TYPE

Grain

NAME

ORIGIN

TYPE

ROASTED/TOASTED

○ WHEAT ___%
○ BARLEY ___%
○ MALT ___%
○ RYE ___%
○ CORN ___%
○ OATS ___%
○ RICE ___%
○ OTHER ___%

SPECIFIC PROPERTIES

Hops

VARIETY

SPECIFIC PROPERTIES

% AMOUNT

ORIGIN/NAME

Sugar

GRANULATED SUGAR

BROWN SUGAR

HONEY

MAPLE SYRUP

CORN SYRUP

MALT

MOLASSES

OTHER

Other Flavorings

TYPE

AMOUNT

USED FOR

ADDED DURING

NOTES

Brewing Log

DATE BREWED ______________________

BATCH SIZE ______________________

TASTING NOTES ______________________

____

____

BEGINNING SPECIFIC GRAVITY ________

FINAL SPECIFIC GRAVITY ________

_____ % ALCOHOL ________

Boil + Mash

TEMPERATURE OF GRAIN ______________

TEMPERATURE OF TUN ______________

BOIL TIME ______________

COOLING TIME & TEMPERATURE ______________

Hops added

BOIL TIME ______________

COOLING TIME & TEMPERATURE ______________

SPECIFIC GRAVITY ______________

Yeast added

TEMPERATURE ______________

LENGTH OF FERMENT ______________

BOTTLING GRAVITY ______________

TYPE OF VESSEL ______________

PRIMER & AMOUNT ______________

Storing and Aging

AGED FOR ______________

STORAGE TEMPERATURE ______________

NOTES ______________________

Tasting and Visual Notes

_____ OG _____ SRM

_____ ABV _____ IBUs

APPEARANCE ______________________

AROMA ______________________

FLAVOR ______________________

FEEL ______________________

OVERALL ______________________

WHAT WORKED?

____

____

____

WHAT DIDN'T?

____

____

____

NAME TYPE
PROPERTIES I'M GOING FOR
FORM
NOTES
FLAVOR/AROMA/PROCESS

Ingredients

Yeast

NAME

MANUFACTURER

LAST CULTURED

Water

pH TREATMENT ○ YES ○ NO

TYPE

Grain

NAME

ORIGIN

TYPE

ROASTED/TOASTED

○ WHEAT ____% ○ CORN ____%
○ BARLEY ____% ○ OATS ____%
○ MALT ____% ○ RICE ____%
○ RYE ____% ○ OTHER ____%

SPECIFIC PROPERTIES

Hops

VARIETY

SPECIFIC PROPERTIES

% AMOUNT

ORIGIN/NAME

Sugar

GRANULATED SUGAR

BROWN SUGAR

HONEY

MAPLE SYRUP

CORN SYRUP

MALT

MOLASSES

OTHER

Other Flavorings

TYPE

AMOUNT

USED FOR

ADDED DURING

NOTES

Brewing Log

DATE BREWED ______

BATCH SIZE ______

TASTING NOTES ______

______

______

BEGINNING SPECIFIC GRAVITY ______

FINAL SPECIFIC GRAVITY ______

______ % ALCOHOL ______

Boil + Mash

TEMPERATURE OF GRAIN ______

TEMPERATURE OF TUN ______

BOIL TIME ______

COOLING TIME & TEMPERATURE ______

Hops added

BOIL TIME ______

COOLING TIME & TEMPERATURE ______

SPECIFIC GRAVITY ______

Yeast added

TEMPERATURE ______

LENGTH OF FERMENT ______

BOTTLING GRAVITY ______

TYPE OF VESSEL ______

PRIMER & AMOUNT ______

Storing and Aging

AGED FOR ______

STORAGE TEMPERATURE ______

NOTES ______

Tasting and Visual Notes

______ OG ______ SRM

______ ABV ______ IBUs

APPEARANCE ______

AROMA ______

FLAVOR ______

FEEL ______

OVERALL ______

WHAT WORKED?

______

WHAT DIDN'T?

______

NAME ______ TYPE ______

PROPERTIES I'M GOING FOR ______

FORM ______

NOTES ______

FLAVOR/AROMA/PROCESS ______

Ingredients

Yeast

NAME ______

MANUFACTURER ______

LAST CULTURED ______

Water

pH TREATMENT ○ YES ○ NO

TYPE ______

Grain

NAME ______

ORIGIN ______

TYPE ______

ROASTED/TOASTED ______

○ WHEAT ____%   ○ CORN ____%

○ BARLEY ____%   ○ OATS ____%

○ MALT ____%   ○ RICE ____%

○ RYE ____%   ○ OTHER ____%

SPECIFIC PROPERTIES ______

Hops

VARIETY ______

SPECIFIC PROPERTIES ______

% AMOUNT ______

ORIGIN/NAME ______

Sugar

GRANULATED SUGAR ______

BROWN SUGAR ______

HONEY ______

MAPLE SYRUP ______

CORN SYRUP ______

MALT ______

MOLASSES ______

OTHER ______

Other Flavorings

TYPE ______

AMOUNT ______

USED FOR ______

ADDED DURING ______

NOTES ______

Brewing Log

DATE BREWED ______

BATCH SIZE ______

TASTING NOTES ______

BEGINNING SPECIFIC GRAVITY ______

FINAL SPECIFIC GRAVITY ______

______ % ALCOHOL ______

Boil + Mash

TEMPERATURE OF GRAIN ______

TEMPERATURE OF TUN ______

BOIL TIME ______

COOLING TIME & TEMPERATURE ______

Hops added

BOIL TIME ______

COOLING TIME & TEMPERATURE ______

SPECIFIC GRAVITY ______

Yeast added

TEMPERATURE ______

LENGTH OF FERMENT ______

BOTTLING GRAVITY ______

TYPE OF VESSEL ______

PRIMER & AMOUNT ______

Storing and Aging

AGED FOR ______

STORAGE TEMPERATURE ______

NOTES ______

Tasting and Visual Notes

______ OG ______ SRM

______ ABV ______ IBUs

APPEARANCE ______

AROMA ______

FLAVOR ______

FEEL ______

OVERALL ______

WHAT WORKED?

WHAT DIDN'T?

NAME | TYPE

PROPERTIES I'M GOING FOR

FORM

NOTES

FLAVOR/AROMA/PROCESS

Ingredients

Yeast

NAME

MANUFACTURER

LAST CULTURED

Water

pH TREATMENT ◯ YES ◯ NO

TYPE

Grain

NAME

ORIGIN

TYPE

ROASTED/TOASTED

- ◯ WHEAT ____%
- ◯ BARLEY ____%
- ◯ MALT ____%
- ◯ RYE ____%
- ◯ CORN ____%
- ◯ OATS ____%
- ◯ RICE ____%
- ◯ OTHER ____%

SPECIFIC PROPERTIES

Hops

VARIETY

SPECIFIC PROPERTIES

% AMOUNT

ORIGIN/NAME

Sugar

GRANULATED SUGAR

BROWN SUGAR

HONEY

MAPLE SYRUP

CORN SYRUP

MALT

MOLASSES

OTHER

Other Flavorings

TYPE

AMOUNT

USED FOR

ADDED DURING

NOTES

Brewing Log

DATE BREWED ______

BATCH SIZE ______

TASTING NOTES ______

BEGINNING SPECIFIC GRAVITY ______

FINAL SPECIFIC GRAVITY ______

______ % ALCOHOL ______

Boil + Mash

TEMPERATURE OF GRAIN ______

TEMPERATURE OF TUN ______

BOIL TIME ______

COOLING TIME & TEMPERATURE ______

Hops added

BOIL TIME ______

COOLING TIME & TEMPERATURE ______

SPECIFIC GRAVITY ______

Yeast added

TEMPERATURE ______

LENGTH OF FERMENT ______

BOTTLING GRAVITY ______

TYPE OF VESSEL ______

PRIMER & AMOUNT ______

Storing and Aging

AGED FOR ______

STORAGE TEMPERATURE ______

NOTES ______

Tasting and Visual Notes

______ OG ______ SRM

______ ABV ______ IBUs

APPEARANCE ______

AROMA ______

FLAVOR ______

FEEL ______

OVERALL ______

WHAT WORKED?

WHAT DIDN'T?

NAME

TYPE

PROPERTIES I'M GOING FOR

FORM

NOTES

FLAVOR/AROMA/PROCESS

Ingredients

Yeast

NAME

MANUFACTURER

LAST CULTURED

Water

pH TREATMENT ◯ YES ◯ NO

TYPE

Grain

NAME

ORIGIN

TYPE

ROASTED/TOASTED

◯ WHEAT ____%
◯ BARLEY ____%
◯ MALT ____%
◯ RYE ____%
◯ CORN ____%
◯ OATS ____%
◯ RICE ____%
◯ OTHER ____%

SPECIFIC PROPERTIES

Hops

VARIETY

SPECIFIC PROPERTIES

% AMOUNT

ORIGIN/NAME

Sugar

GRANULATED SUGAR

BROWN SUGAR

HONEY

MAPLE SYRUP

CORN SYRUP

MALT

MOLASSES

OTHER

Other Flavorings

TYPE

AMOUNT

USED FOR

ADDED DURING

NOTES

Brewing Log

DATE BREWED ______________________

BATCH SIZE ______________________

TASTING NOTES ______________________

____

____

BEGINNING SPECIFIC GRAVITY __________

FINAL SPECIFIC GRAVITY __________

______ % ALCOHOL __________

Boil + Mash

TEMPERATURE OF GRAIN ______________

TEMPERATURE OF TUN ______________

BOIL TIME ______________

COOLING TIME & TEMPERATURE ______________

Hops added

BOIL TIME ______________

COOLING TIME & TEMPERATURE ______________

SPECIFIC GRAVITY ______________

Yeast added

TEMPERATURE ______________

LENGTH OF FERMENT ______________

BOTTLING GRAVITY ______________

TYPE OF VESSEL ______________

PRIMER & AMOUNT ______________

Storing and Aging

AGED FOR ______________

STORAGE TEMPERATURE ______________

NOTES ______________________

Tasting and Visual Notes

______ OG ______ SRM

______ ABV ______ IBUs

APPEARANCE ______________________

AROMA ______________________

FLAVOR ______________________

FEEL ______________________

OVERALL ______________________

WHAT WORKED?

____

____

____

WHAT DIDN'T?

____

____

____

NAME ____ TYPE ____
PROPERTIES I'M GOING FOR ____
____
FORM ____
NOTES ____
____
FLAVOR/AROMA/PROCESS ____

Ingredients

Yeast

NAME ____
MANUFACTURER ____
LAST CULTURED ____

Grain

NAME ____
ORIGIN ____
TYPE ____
ROASTED/TOASTED ____

- WHEAT ____%
- BARLEY ____%
- MALT ____%
- RYE ____%
- CORN ____%
- OATS ____%
- RICE ____%
- OTHER ____%

SPECIFIC PROPERTIES ____

Sugar

GRANULATED SUGAR ____
BROWN SUGAR ____
HONEY ____
MAPLE SYRUP ____
CORN SYRUP ____
MALT ____
MOLASSES ____
OTHER ____

Water

pH TREATMENT ○ YES ○ NO
TYPE ____

Hops

VARIETY ____
SPECIFIC PROPERTIES ____
____
____
% AMOUNT ____
ORIGIN/NAME ____

Other Flavorings

TYPE ____
AMOUNT ____
USED FOR ____
ADDED DURING ____

NOTES ____
____
____
____
____
____
____

Brewing Log

DATE BREWED ____________________

BATCH SIZE ____________________

TASTING NOTES ____________________

BEGINNING SPECIFIC GRAVITY ________

FINAL SPECIFIC GRAVITY ________

______ % ALCOHOL ________

Boil + Mash

TEMPERATURE OF GRAIN ________

TEMPERATURE OF TUN ________

BOIL TIME ________

COOLING TIME & TEMPERATURE ________

Hops added

BOIL TIME ________

COOLING TIME & TEMPERATURE ________

SPECIFIC GRAVITY ________

Yeast added

TEMPERATURE ________

LENGTH OF FERMENT ________

BOTTLING GRAVITY ________

TYPE OF VESSEL ________

PRIMER & AMOUNT ________

Storing and Aging

AGED FOR ________

STORAGE TEMPERATURE ________

NOTES ________

Tasting and Visual Notes

______ OG ______ SRM

______ ABV ______ IBUs

APPEARANCE ________

AROMA ________

FLAVOR ________

FEEL ________

OVERALL ________

WHAT WORKED?

WHAT DIDN'T?

NAME ______ TYPE ______

PROPERTIES I'M GOING FOR ______

______

FORM ______

NOTES ______

______

FLAVOR/AROMA/PROCESS ______

Ingredients

Yeast

NAME ______

MANUFACTURER ______

LAST CULTURED ______

Water

pH TREATMENT ○ YES ○ NO

TYPE ______

Grain

NAME ______

ORIGIN ______

TYPE ______

ROASTED/TOASTED ______

○ WHEAT ______% ○ CORN ______%

○ BARLEY ______% ○ OATS ______%

○ MALT ______% ○ RICE ______%

○ RYE ______% ○ OTHER ______%

SPECIFIC PROPERTIES ______

Hops

VARIETY ______

SPECIFIC PROPERTIES ______

______

______

% AMOUNT ______

ORIGIN/NAME ______

Sugar

GRANULATED SUGAR ______

BROWN SUGAR ______

HONEY ______

MAPLE SYRUP ______

CORN SYRUP ______

MALT ______

MOLASSES ______

OTHER ______

Other Flavorings

TYPE ______

AMOUNT ______

USED FOR ______

ADDED DURING ______

NOTES ______

______

______

______

______

______

______

Brewing Log

DATE BREWED ______

BATCH SIZE ______

TASTING NOTES ______

BEGINNING SPECIFIC GRAVITY ______

FINAL SPECIFIC GRAVITY ______

______ % ALCOHOL ______

Boil + Mash

TEMPERATURE OF GRAIN ______

TEMPERATURE OF TUN ______

BOIL TIME ______

COOLING TIME & TEMPERATURE ______

Hops added

BOIL TIME ______

COOLING TIME & TEMPERATURE ______

SPECIFIC GRAVITY ______

Yeast added

TEMPERATURE ______

LENGTH OF FERMENT ______

BOTTLING GRAVITY ______

TYPE OF VESSEL ______

PRIMER & AMOUNT ______

Storing and Aging

AGED FOR ______

STORAGE TEMPERATURE ______

NOTES ______

Tasting and Visual Notes

______ OG ______ SRM

______ ABV ______ IBUs

APPEARANCE ______

AROMA ______

FLAVOR ______

FEEL ______

OVERALL ______

WHAT WORKED?

WHAT DIDN'T?

NAME ______ TYPE ______

PROPERTIES I'M GOING FOR ______

FORM ______

NOTES ______

FLAVOR/AROMA/PROCESS ______

Ingredients

Yeast

NAME ______

MANUFACTURER ______

LAST CULTURED ______

Water

pH TREATMENT ○ YES ○ NO

TYPE ______

Grain

NAME ______

ORIGIN ______

TYPE ______

ROASTED/TOASTED ______

○ WHEAT ____% ○ CORN ____%

○ BARLEY ____% ○ OATS ____%

○ MALT ____% ○ RICE ____%

○ RYE ____% ○ OTHER ____%

SPECIFIC PROPERTIES ______

Hops

VARIETY ______

SPECIFIC PROPERTIES ______

% AMOUNT ______

ORIGIN/NAME ______

Sugar

GRANULATED SUGAR ______

BROWN SUGAR ______

HONEY ______

MAPLE SYRUP ______

CORN SYRUP ______

MALT ______

MOLASSES ______

OTHER ______

Other Flavorings

TYPE ______

AMOUNT ______

USED FOR ______

ADDED DURING ______

NOTES ______

Brewing Log

DATE BREWED ____________
BATCH SIZE ____________
TASTING NOTES ____________

BEGINNING SPECIFIC GRAVITY ____________
FINAL SPECIFIC GRAVITY ____________
______ % ALCOHOL ____________

Boil + Mash

TEMPERATURE OF GRAIN ____________
TEMPERATURE OF TUN ____________
BOIL TIME ____________
COOLING TIME & TEMPERATURE ____________

Hops added

BOIL TIME ____________
COOLING TIME & TEMPERATURE ____________
SPECIFIC GRAVITY ____________

Yeast added

TEMPERATURE ____________
LENGTH OF FERMENT ____________
BOTTLING GRAVITY ____________
TYPE OF VESSEL ____________
PRIMER & AMOUNT ____________

Storing and Aging

AGED FOR ____________
STORAGE TEMPERATURE ____________

NOTES ____________

Tasting and Visual Notes

______ OG ______ SRM
______ ABV ______ IBUs

APPEARANCE ____________
AROMA ____________
FLAVOR ____________
FEEL ____________
OVERALL ____________

WHAT WORKED?

WHAT DIDN'T?

NAME ____ TYPE ____
PROPERTIES I'M GOING FOR ____
FORM ____
NOTES ____
FLAVOR/AROMA/PROCESS ____

Ingredients

Yeast

NAME ____
MANUFACTURER ____
LAST CULTURED ____

Water

pH TREATMENT ○ YES ○ NO
TYPE ____

Grain

NAME ____
ORIGIN ____
TYPE ____
ROASTED/TOASTED ____

○ WHEAT ____%
○ BARLEY ____%
○ MALT ____%
○ RYE ____%
○ CORN ____%
○ OATS ____%
○ RICE ____%
○ OTHER ____%

SPECIFIC PROPERTIES ____

Hops

VARIETY ____
SPECIFIC PROPERTIES ____
% AMOUNT ____
ORIGIN/NAME ____

Sugar

GRANULATED SUGAR ____
BROWN SUGAR ____
HONEY ____
MAPLE SYRUP ____
CORN SYRUP ____
MALT ____
MOLASSES ____
OTHER ____

Other Flavorings

TYPE ____
AMOUNT ____
USED FOR ____
ADDED DURING ____

NOTES ____

Brewing Log

DATE BREWED ____________________

BATCH SIZE ____________________

TASTING NOTES ____________________

BEGINNING SPECIFIC GRAVITY __________

FINAL SPECIFIC GRAVITY __________

______ % ALCOHOL __________

Boil + Mash

TEMPERATURE OF GRAIN __________

TEMPERATURE OF TUN __________

BOIL TIME __________

COOLING TIME & TEMPERATURE __________

Hops added

BOIL TIME __________

COOLING TIME & TEMPERATURE __________

SPECIFIC GRAVITY __________

Yeast added

TEMPERATURE __________

LENGTH OF FERMENT __________

BOTTLING GRAVITY __________

TYPE OF VESSEL __________

PRIMER & AMOUNT __________

Storing and Aging

AGED FOR __________

STORAGE TEMPERATURE __________

NOTES ____________________

Tasting and Visual Notes

______ OG ______ SRM

______ ABV ______ IBUs

APPEARANCE ____________________

AROMA ____________________

FLAVOR ____________________

FEEL ____________________

OVERALL ____________________

WHAT WORKED?

WHAT DIDN'T?

NAME ____ TYPE ____
PROPERTIES I'M GOING FOR ____

FORM ____
NOTES ____

FLAVOR/AROMA/PROCESS ____

Ingredients

Yeast

NAME ____
MANUFACTURER ____
LAST CULTURED ____

Water

pH TREATMENT ○ YES ○ NO
TYPE ____

Grain

NAME ____
ORIGIN ____
TYPE ____
ROASTED/TOASTED ____

○ WHEAT ____% ○ CORN ____%
○ BARLEY ____% ○ OATS ____%
○ MALT ____% ○ RICE ____%
○ RYE ____% ○ OTHER ____%

SPECIFIC PROPERTIES ____

Hops

VARIETY ____
SPECIFIC PROPERTIES ____

% AMOUNT ____
ORIGIN/NAME ____

Sugar

GRANULATED SUGAR ____
BROWN SUGAR ____
HONEY ____
MAPLE SYRUP ____
CORN SYRUP ____
MALT ____
MOLASSES ____
OTHER ____

Other Flavorings

TYPE ____
AMOUNT ____
USED FOR ____
ADDED DURING ____

NOTES ____

Brewing Log

DATE BREWED ______

BATCH SIZE ______

TASTING NOTES ______

______

______

BEGINNING SPECIFIC GRAVITY ______

FINAL SPECIFIC GRAVITY ______

______ % ALCOHOL ______

Boil + Mash

TEMPERATURE OF GRAIN ______

TEMPERATURE OF TUN ______

BOIL TIME ______

COOLING TIME & TEMPERATURE ______

Hops added

BOIL TIME ______

COOLING TIME & TEMPERATURE ______

SPECIFIC GRAVITY ______

Yeast added

TEMPERATURE ______

LENGTH OF FERMENT ______

BOTTLING GRAVITY ______

TYPE OF VESSEL ______

PRIMER & AMOUNT ______

Storing and Aging

AGED FOR ______

STORAGE TEMPERATURE ______

NOTES ______

Tasting and Visual Notes

______ OG ______ SRM

______ ABV ______ IBUs

APPEARANCE ______

AROMA ______

FLAVOR ______

FEEL ______

OVERALL ______

WHAT WORKED?

______

WHAT DIDN'T?

______

NAME ______ TYPE ______
PROPERTIES I'M GOING FOR ______
FORM ______
NOTES ______
FLAVOR/AROMA/PROCESS ______

Ingredients

Yeast

NAME ______
MANUFACTURER ______
LAST CULTURED ______

Water

pH TREATMENT ○ YES ○ NO
TYPE ______

Grain

NAME ______
ORIGIN ______
TYPE ______
ROASTED/TOASTED ______

○ WHEAT ___% ○ CORN ___%
○ BARLEY ___% ○ OATS ___%
○ MALT ___% ○ RICE ___%
○ RYE ___% ○ OTHER ___%

SPECIFIC PROPERTIES ______

Hops

VARIETY ______
SPECIFIC PROPERTIES ______
% AMOUNT ______
ORIGIN/NAME ______

Sugar

GRANULATED SUGAR ______
BROWN SUGAR ______
HONEY ______
MAPLE SYRUP ______
CORN SYRUP ______
MALT ______
MOLASSES ______
OTHER ______

Other Flavorings

TYPE ______
AMOUNT ______
USED FOR ______
ADDED DURING ______

NOTES ______

Brewing Log

DATE BREWED ______
BATCH SIZE ______
TASTING NOTES ______

BEGINNING SPECIFIC GRAVITY ______
FINAL SPECIFIC GRAVITY ______
______ % ALCOHOL ______

Boil + Mash

TEMPERATURE OF GRAIN ______
TEMPERATURE OF TUN ______
BOIL TIME ______
COOLING TIME & TEMPERATURE ______

Hops added

BOIL TIME ______
COOLING TIME & TEMPERATURE ______
SPECIFIC GRAVITY ______

Yeast added

TEMPERATURE ______
LENGTH OF FERMENT ______
BOTTLING GRAVITY ______
TYPE OF VESSEL ______
PRIMER & AMOUNT ______

Storing and Aging

AGED FOR ______
STORAGE TEMPERATURE ______

NOTES ______

Tasting and Visual Notes

______ OG ______ SRM
______ ABV ______ IBUs

APPEARANCE ______
AROMA ______
FLAVOR ______
FEEL ______
OVERALL ______

WHAT WORKED?

WHAT DIDN'T?

NAME TYPE
PROPERTIES I'M GOING FOR
FORM
NOTES
FLAVOR/AROMA/PROCESS

Ingredients

Yeast

NAME
MANUFACTURER
LAST CULTURED

Water

pH TREATMENT ○ YES ○ NO
TYPE

Grain

NAME
ORIGIN
TYPE
ROASTED/TOASTED

- ○ WHEAT ____%
- ○ BARLEY ____%
- ○ MALT ____%
- ○ RYE ____%
- ○ CORN ____%
- ○ OATS ____%
- ○ RICE ____%
- ○ OTHER ____%

SPECIFIC PROPERTIES

Hops

VARIETY
SPECIFIC PROPERTIES
% AMOUNT
ORIGIN/NAME

Sugar

GRANULATED SUGAR
BROWN SUGAR
HONEY
MAPLE SYRUP
CORN SYRUP
MALT
MOLASSES
OTHER

Other Flavorings

TYPE
AMOUNT
USED FOR
ADDED DURING

NOTES

Brewing Log

DATE BREWED ______

BATCH SIZE ______

TASTING NOTES ______

______

______

BEGINNING SPECIFIC GRAVITY ______

FINAL SPECIFIC GRAVITY ______

______ % ALCOHOL ______

Boil + Mash

TEMPERATURE OF GRAIN ______

TEMPERATURE OF TUN ______

BOIL TIME ______

COOLING TIME & TEMPERATURE ______

Hops added

BOIL TIME ______

COOLING TIME & TEMPERATURE ______

SPECIFIC GRAVITY ______

Yeast added

TEMPERATURE ______

LENGTH OF FERMENT ______

BOTTLING GRAVITY ______

TYPE OF VESSEL ______

PRIMER & AMOUNT ______

Storing and Aging

AGED FOR ______

STORAGE TEMPERATURE ______

NOTES ______

Tasting and Visual Notes

______ OG ______ SRM

______ ABV ______ IBUs

APPEARANCE ______

AROMA ______

FLAVOR ______

FEEL ______

OVERALL ______

WHAT WORKED?

______

WHAT DIDN'T?

______

NAME ____ TYPE ____
PROPERTIES I'M GOING FOR ____
____
FORM ____
NOTES ____
____
FLAVOR/AROMA/PROCESS ____

Ingredients

Yeast

NAME ____
MANUFACTURER ____
LAST CULTURED ____

Water

pH TREATMENT ○ YES ○ NO
TYPE ____

Grain

NAME ____
ORIGIN ____
TYPE ____
ROASTED/TOASTED ____

○ WHEAT ____% ○ CORN ____%
○ BARLEY ____% ○ OATS ____%
○ MALT ____% ○ RICE ____%
○ RYE ____% ○ OTHER ____%

SPECIFIC PROPERTIES ____

Hops

VARIETY ____
SPECIFIC PROPERTIES ____
____
____
% AMOUNT ____
ORIGIN/NAME ____

Sugar

GRANULATED SUGAR ____
BROWN SUGAR ____
HONEY ____
MAPLE SYRUP ____
CORN SYRUP ____
MALT ____
MOLASSES ____
OTHER ____

Other Flavorings

TYPE ____
AMOUNT ____
USED FOR ____
ADDED DURING ____

NOTES ____
____
____
____
____
____
____

Brewing Log

DATE BREWED ______

BATCH SIZE ______

TASTING NOTES ______

______

______

BEGINNING SPECIFIC GRAVITY ______

FINAL SPECIFIC GRAVITY ______

______ % ALCOHOL ______

Boil + Mash

TEMPERATURE OF GRAIN ______

TEMPERATURE OF TUN ______

BOIL TIME ______

COOLING TIME & TEMPERATURE ______

Hops added

BOIL TIME ______

COOLING TIME & TEMPERATURE ______

SPECIFIC GRAVITY ______

Yeast added

TEMPERATURE ______

LENGTH OF FERMENT ______

BOTTLING GRAVITY ______

TYPE OF VESSEL ______

PRIMER & AMOUNT ______

Storing and Aging

AGED FOR ______

STORAGE TEMPERATURE ______

NOTES ______

Tasting and Visual Notes

______ OG ______ SRM

______ ABV ______ IBUs

APPEARANCE ______

AROMA ______

FLAVOR ______

FEEL ______

OVERALL ______

WHAT WORKED?

______

WHAT DIDN'T?

______

NAME TYPE
PROPERTIES I'M GOING FOR
FORM
NOTES
FLAVOR/AROMA/PROCESS

Ingredients

Yeast
NAME
MANUFACTURER
LAST CULTURED

Grain
NAME
ORIGIN
TYPE
ROASTED/TOASTED

- WHEAT ____%
- BARLEY ____%
- MALT ____%
- RYE ____%
- CORN ____%
- OATS ____%
- RICE ____%
- OTHER ____%

SPECIFIC PROPERTIES

Sugar
GRANULATED SUGAR
BROWN SUGAR
HONEY
MAPLE SYRUP
CORN SYRUP
MALT
MOLASSES
OTHER

Water
pH TREATMENT YES NO
TYPE

Hops
VARIETY
SPECIFIC PROPERTIES
% AMOUNT
ORIGIN/NAME

Other Flavorings
TYPE
AMOUNT
USED FOR
ADDED DURING

NOTES

Brewing Log

DATE BREWED ____________

BATCH SIZE ____________

TASTING NOTES ____________

BEGINNING SPECIFIC GRAVITY ____________

FINAL SPECIFIC GRAVITY ____________

______ % ALCOHOL ____________

Boil + Mash

TEMPERATURE OF GRAIN ____________

TEMPERATURE OF TUN ____________

BOIL TIME ____________

COOLING TIME & TEMPERATURE ____________

Hops added

BOIL TIME ____________

COOLING TIME & TEMPERATURE ____________

SPECIFIC GRAVITY ____________

Yeast added

TEMPERATURE ____________

LENGTH OF FERMENT ____________

BOTTLING GRAVITY ____________

TYPE OF VESSEL ____________

PRIMER & AMOUNT ____________

Storing and Aging

AGED FOR ____________

STORAGE TEMPERATURE ____________

NOTES ____________

Tasting and Visual Notes

______ OG ______ SRM

______ ABV ______ IBUs

APPEARANCE ____________

AROMA ____________

FLAVOR ____________

FEEL ____________

OVERALL ____________

WHAT WORKED?

WHAT DIDN'T?

NAME TYPE
PROPERTIES I'M GOING FOR
FORM
NOTES
FLAVOR/AROMA/PROCESS

Ingredients

Yeast

NAME
MANUFACTURER
LAST CULTURED

Grain

NAME
ORIGIN
TYPE
ROASTED/TOASTED

- WHEAT ____%
- BARLEY ____%
- MALT ____%
- RYE ____%
- CORN ____%
- OATS ____%
- RICE ____%
- OTHER ____%

SPECIFIC PROPERTIES

Sugar

GRANULATED SUGAR
BROWN SUGAR
HONEY
MAPLE SYRUP
CORN SYRUP
MALT
MOLASSES
OTHER

Water

pH TREATMENT ○ YES ○ NO
TYPE

Hops

VARIETY
SPECIFIC PROPERTIES
% AMOUNT
ORIGIN/NAME

Other Flavorings

TYPE
AMOUNT
USED FOR
ADDED DURING

NOTES

Brewing Log

DATE BREWED ____________________

BATCH SIZE ____________________

TASTING NOTES ____________________

____

____

BEGINNING SPECIFIC GRAVITY __________

FINAL SPECIFIC GRAVITY __________

______ % ALCOHOL __________

Boil + Mash

TEMPERATURE OF GRAIN ____________________

TEMPERATURE OF TUN ____________________

BOIL TIME ____________________

COOLING TIME & TEMPERATURE ____________________

Hops added

BOIL TIME ____________________

COOLING TIME & TEMPERATURE ____________________

SPECIFIC GRAVITY ____________________

Yeast added

TEMPERATURE ____________________

LENGTH OF FERMENT ____________________

BOTTLING GRAVITY ____________________

TYPE OF VESSEL ____________________

PRIMER & AMOUNT ____________________

Storing and Aging

AGED FOR ____________________

STORAGE TEMPERATURE ____________________

NOTES ____________________

Tasting and Visual Notes

______ OG ______ SRM

______ ABV ______ IBUs

APPEARANCE ____________________

AROMA ____________________

FLAVOR ____________________

FEEL ____________________

OVERALL ____________________

WHAT WORKED?

____

____

____

WHAT DIDN'T?

____

____

____

NAME TYPE

PROPERTIES I'M GOING FOR

FORM

NOTES

FLAVOR/AROMA/PROCESS

Ingredients

Yeast

NAME

MANUFACTURER

LAST CULTURED

Grain

NAME

ORIGIN

TYPE

ROASTED/TOASTED

WHEAT ____%
CORN ____%
BARLEY ____%
OATS ____%
MALT ____%
RICE ____%
RYE ____%
OTHER ____%

SPECIFIC PROPERTIES

Sugar

GRANULATED SUGAR

BROWN SUGAR

HONEY

MAPLE SYRUP

CORN SYRUP

MALT

MOLASSES

OTHER

Water

pH TREATMENT YES NO

TYPE

Hops

VARIETY

SPECIFIC PROPERTIES

% AMOUNT

ORIGIN/NAME

Other Flavorings

TYPE

AMOUNT

USED FOR

ADDED DURING

NOTES

Brewing Log

DATE BREWED ______
BATCH SIZE ______
TASTING NOTES ______

BEGINNING SPECIFIC GRAVITY ______
FINAL SPECIFIC GRAVITY ______
______ % ALCOHOL ______

Boil + Mash

TEMPERATURE OF GRAIN ______
TEMPERATURE OF TUN ______
BOIL TIME ______
COOLING TIME & TEMPERATURE ______

Hops added

BOIL TIME ______
COOLING TIME & TEMPERATURE ______
SPECIFIC GRAVITY ______

Yeast added

TEMPERATURE ______
LENGTH OF FERMENT ______
BOTTLING GRAVITY ______
TYPE OF VESSEL ______
PRIMER & AMOUNT ______

Storing and Aging

AGED FOR ______
STORAGE TEMPERATURE ______

NOTES ______

Tasting and Visual Notes

______ OG ______ SRM
______ ABV ______ IBUs

APPEARANCE ______
AROMA ______
FLAVOR ______
FEEL ______
OVERALL ______

WHAT WORKED?

WHAT DIDN'T?

NAME ____ TYPE ____
PROPERTIES I'M GOING FOR ____
FORM ____
NOTES ____
FLAVOR/AROMA/PROCESS ____

Ingredients

Yeast

NAME ____
MANUFACTURER ____
LAST CULTURED ____

Water

pH TREATMENT ○ YES ○ NO
TYPE ____

Grain

NAME ____
ORIGIN ____
TYPE ____
ROASTED/TOASTED ____

- ○ WHEAT ____%
- ○ BARLEY ____%
- ○ MALT ____%
- ○ RYE ____%
- ○ CORN ____%
- ○ OATS ____%
- ○ RICE ____%
- ○ OTHER ____%

SPECIFIC PROPERTIES ____

Hops

VARIETY ____
SPECIFIC PROPERTIES ____
% AMOUNT ____
ORIGIN/NAME ____

Sugar

GRANULATED SUGAR ____
BROWN SUGAR ____
HONEY ____
MAPLE SYRUP ____
CORN SYRUP ____
MALT ____
MOLASSES ____
OTHER ____

Other Flavorings

TYPE ____
AMOUNT ____
USED FOR ____
ADDED DURING ____

NOTES ____

Brewing Log

DATE BREWED ____________________

BATCH SIZE ____________________

TASTING NOTES ____________________

BEGINNING SPECIFIC GRAVITY ________

FINAL SPECIFIC GRAVITY ________

______ % ALCOHOL ________

Boil + Mash

TEMPERATURE OF GRAIN ____________

TEMPERATURE OF TUN ____________

BOIL TIME ____________

COOLING TIME & TEMPERATURE ____________

Hops added

BOIL TIME ____________

COOLING TIME & TEMPERATURE ____________

SPECIFIC GRAVITY ____________

Yeast added

TEMPERATURE ____________

LENGTH OF FERMENT ____________

BOTTLING GRAVITY ____________

TYPE OF VESSEL ____________

PRIMER & AMOUNT ____________

Storing and Aging

AGED FOR ____________

STORAGE TEMPERATURE ____________

NOTES ____________________

Tasting and Visual Notes

______ OG ______ SRM

______ ABV ______ IBUs

APPEARANCE ____________________

AROMA ____________________

FLAVOR ____________________

FEEL ____________________

OVERALL ____________________

WHAT WORKED?

WHAT DIDN'T?

NAME ______ TYPE ______
PROPERTIES I'M GOING FOR ______
FORM ______
NOTES ______
FLAVOR/AROMA/PROCESS ______

Ingredients

Yeast

NAME ______
MANUFACTURER ______
LAST CULTURED ______

Water

pH TREATMENT ○ YES ○ NO
TYPE ______

Grain

NAME ______
ORIGIN ______
TYPE ______
ROASTED/TOASTED ______

○ WHEAT ____% ○ CORN ____%
○ BARLEY ____% ○ OATS ____%
○ MALT ____% ○ RICE ____%
○ RYE ____% ○ OTHER ____%

SPECIFIC PROPERTIES ______

Hops

VARIETY ______
SPECIFIC PROPERTIES ______
% AMOUNT ______
ORIGIN/NAME ______

Sugar

GRANULATED SUGAR ______
BROWN SUGAR ______
HONEY ______
MAPLE SYRUP ______
CORN SYRUP ______
MALT ______
MOLASSES ______
OTHER ______

Other Flavorings

TYPE ______
AMOUNT ______
USED FOR ______
ADDED DURING ______

NOTES ______

Brewing Log

DATE BREWED ______

BATCH SIZE ______

TASTING NOTES ______

______

______

BEGINNING SPECIFIC GRAVITY ______

FINAL SPECIFIC GRAVITY ______

______ % ALCOHOL ______

Boil + Mash

TEMPERATURE OF GRAIN ______

TEMPERATURE OF TUN ______

BOIL TIME ______

COOLING TIME & TEMPERATURE ______

Hops added

BOIL TIME ______

COOLING TIME & TEMPERATURE ______

SPECIFIC GRAVITY ______

Yeast added

TEMPERATURE ______

LENGTH OF FERMENT ______

BOTTLING GRAVITY ______

TYPE OF VESSEL ______

PRIMER & AMOUNT ______

Storing and Aging

AGED FOR ______

STORAGE TEMPERATURE ______

NOTES ______

Tasting and Visual Notes

______ OG ______ SRM

______ ABV ______ IBUs

APPEARANCE ______

AROMA ______

FLAVOR ______

FEEL ______

OVERALL ______

WHAT WORKED?

______

WHAT DIDN'T?

______

NAME ______ TYPE ______
PROPERTIES I'M GOING FOR ______
______
FORM ______
NOTES ______
______
FLAVOR/AROMA/PROCESS ______

Ingredients

Yeast
NAME ______
MANUFACTURER ______
LAST CULTURED ______

Water
pH TREATMENT ○ YES ○ NO
TYPE ______

Grain
NAME ______
ORIGIN ______
TYPE ______
ROASTED/TOASTED ______

○ WHEAT ______%
○ BARLEY ______%
○ MALT ______%
○ RYE ______%
○ CORN ______%
○ OATS ______%
○ RICE ______%
○ OTHER ______%

SPECIFIC PROPERTIES ______

Hops
VARIETY ______
SPECIFIC PROPERTIES ______
______
______
% AMOUNT ______
ORIGIN/NAME ______

Sugar
GRANULATED SUGAR ______
BROWN SUGAR ______
HONEY ______
MAPLE SYRUP ______
CORN SYRUP ______
MALT ______
MOLASSES ______
OTHER ______

Other Flavorings
TYPE ______
AMOUNT ______
USED FOR ______
ADDED DURING ______

NOTES ______
______
______
______
______
______
______

Brewing Log

DATE BREWED ______

BATCH SIZE ______

TASTING NOTES ______

______

______

BEGINNING SPECIFIC GRAVITY ______

FINAL SPECIFIC GRAVITY ______

______ % ALCOHOL ______

Boil + Mash

TEMPERATURE OF GRAIN ______

TEMPERATURE OF TUN ______

BOIL TIME ______

COOLING TIME & TEMPERATURE ______

Hops added

BOIL TIME ______

COOLING TIME & TEMPERATURE ______

SPECIFIC GRAVITY ______

Yeast added

TEMPERATURE ______

LENGTH OF FERMENT ______

BOTTLING GRAVITY ______

TYPE OF VESSEL ______

PRIMER & AMOUNT ______

Storing and Aging

AGED FOR ______

STORAGE TEMPERATURE ______

NOTES ______

Tasting and Visual Notes

______ OG ______ SRM

______ ABV ______ IBUs

APPEARANCE ______

AROMA ______

FLAVOR ______

FEEL ______

OVERALL ______

WHAT WORKED?

______

WHAT DIDN'T?

______

NAME

TYPE

PROPERTIES I'M GOING FOR

FORM

NOTES

FLAVOR/AROMA/PROCESS

Ingredients

Yeast

NAME

MANUFACTURER

LAST CULTURED

Water

pH TREATMENT YES NO

TYPE

Grain

NAME

ORIGIN

TYPE

ROASTED/TOASTED

WHEAT ___%
CORN ___%
BARLEY ___%
OATS ___%
MALT ___%
RICE ___%
RYE ___%
OTHER ___%

SPECIFIC PROPERTIES

Hops

VARIETY

SPECIFIC PROPERTIES

% AMOUNT

ORIGIN/NAME

Sugar

GRANULATED SUGAR

BROWN SUGAR

HONEY

MAPLE SYRUP

CORN SYRUP

MALT

MOLASSES

OTHER

Other Flavorings

TYPE

AMOUNT

USED FOR

ADDED DURING

NOTES

Brewing Log

DATE BREWED

BATCH SIZE

TASTING NOTES

BEGINNING SPECIFIC GRAVITY

FINAL SPECIFIC GRAVITY

% ALCOHOL

Boil + Mash

TEMPERATURE OF GRAIN

TEMPERATURE OF TUN

BOIL TIME

COOLING TIME & TEMPERATURE

Hops added

BOIL TIME

COOLING TIME & TEMPERATURE

SPECIFIC GRAVITY

Yeast added

TEMPERATURE

LENGTH OF FERMENT

BOTTLING GRAVITY

TYPE OF VESSEL

PRIMER & AMOUNT

Storing and Aging

AGED FOR

STORAGE TEMPERATURE

NOTES

Tasting and Visual Notes

OG

SRM

ABV

IBUs

APPEARANCE

AROMA

FLAVOR

FEEL

OVERALL

WHAT WORKED?

WHAT DIDN'T?

NAME | TYPE
PROPERTIES I'M GOING FOR
FORM
NOTES
FLAVOR/AROMA/PROCESS

Ingredients

Yeast

NAME ______

MANUFACTURER ______

LAST CULTURED ______

Water

pH TREATMENT ○ YES ○ NO

TYPE ______

Grain

NAME ______

ORIGIN ______

TYPE ______

ROASTED/TOASTED ______

○ WHEAT ____% ○ CORN ____%
○ BARLEY ____% ○ OATS ____%
○ MALT ____% ○ RICE ____%
○ RYE ____% ○ OTHER ____%

SPECIFIC PROPERTIES ______

Hops

VARIETY ______

SPECIFIC PROPERTIES ______

% AMOUNT ______

ORIGIN/NAME ______

Sugar

GRANULATED SUGAR ______

BROWN SUGAR ______

HONEY ______

MAPLE SYRUP ______

CORN SYRUP ______

MALT ______

MOLASSES ______

OTHER ______

Other Flavorings

TYPE ______

AMOUNT ______

USED FOR ______

ADDED DURING ______

NOTES ______

Brewing Log

DATE BREWED ______

BATCH SIZE ______

TASTING NOTES ______

BEGINNING SPECIFIC GRAVITY ______

FINAL SPECIFIC GRAVITY ______

______ % ALCOHOL ______

Boil + Mash

TEMPERATURE OF GRAIN ______

TEMPERATURE OF TUN ______

BOIL TIME ______

COOLING TIME & TEMPERATURE ______

Hops added

BOIL TIME ______

COOLING TIME & TEMPERATURE ______

SPECIFIC GRAVITY ______

Yeast added

TEMPERATURE ______

LENGTH OF FERMENT ______

BOTTLING GRAVITY ______

TYPE OF VESSEL ______

PRIMER & AMOUNT ______

Storing and Aging

AGED FOR ______

STORAGE TEMPERATURE ______

NOTES ______

Tasting and Visual Notes

______ OG ______ SRM

______ ABV ______ IBUs

APPEARANCE ______

AROMA ______

FLAVOR ______

FEEL ______

OVERALL ______

WHAT WORKED?

WHAT DIDN'T?

NAME ______ TYPE ______
PROPERTIES I'M GOING FOR ______
______
FORM ______
NOTES ______
______
FLAVOR/AROMA/PROCESS ______

Ingredients

Yeast

NAME ______
MANUFACTURER ______
LAST CULTURED ______

Water

pH TREATMENT ○ YES ○ NO
TYPE ______

Grain

NAME ______
ORIGIN ______
TYPE ______
ROASTED/TOASTED ______

○ WHEAT ____% ○ CORN ____%
○ BARLEY ____% ○ OATS ____%
○ MALT ____% ○ RICE ____%
○ RYE ____% ○ OTHER ____%

SPECIFIC PROPERTIES ______

Hops

VARIETY ______
SPECIFIC PROPERTIES ______
______
______
% AMOUNT ______
ORIGIN/NAME ______

Sugar

GRANULATED SUGAR ______
BROWN SUGAR ______
HONEY ______
MAPLE SYRUP ______
CORN SYRUP ______
MALT ______
MOLASSES ______
OTHER ______

Other Flavorings

TYPE ______
AMOUNT ______
USED FOR ______
ADDED DURING ______

NOTES ______

Brewing Log

DATE BREWED ____________

BATCH SIZE ____________

TASTING NOTES ____________

BEGINNING SPECIFIC GRAVITY ____________

FINAL SPECIFIC GRAVITY ____________

____ % ALCOHOL ____________

Boil + Mash

TEMPERATURE OF GRAIN ____________

TEMPERATURE OF TUN ____________

BOIL TIME ____________

COOLING TIME & TEMPERATURE ____________

Hops added

BOIL TIME ____________

COOLING TIME & TEMPERATURE ____________

SPECIFIC GRAVITY ____________

Yeast added

TEMPERATURE ____________

LENGTH OF FERMENT ____________

BOTTLING GRAVITY ____________

TYPE OF VESSEL ____________

PRIMER & AMOUNT ____________

Storing and Aging

AGED FOR ____________

STORAGE TEMPERATURE ____________

NOTES ____________

Tasting and Visual Notes

____ OG ____ SRM

____ ABV ____ IBUs

APPEARANCE ____________

AROMA ____________

FLAVOR ____________

FEEL ____________

OVERALL ____________

WHAT WORKED?

WHAT DIDN'T?

NAME ____ TYPE ____
PROPERTIES I'M GOING FOR ____
____
FORM ____
NOTES ____
____
FLAVOR/AROMA/PROCESS ____

Ingredients

Yeast

NAME ____
MANUFACTURER ____
LAST CULTURED ____

Grain

NAME ____
ORIGIN ____
TYPE ____
ROASTED/TOASTED ____

- WHEAT ____%
- BARLEY ____%
- MALT ____%
- RYE ____%
- CORN ____%
- OATS ____%
- RICE ____%
- OTHER ____%

SPECIFIC PROPERTIES ____

Sugar

GRANULATED SUGAR ____
BROWN SUGAR ____
HONEY ____
MAPLE SYRUP ____
CORN SYRUP ____
MALT ____
MOLASSES ____
OTHER ____

Water

pH TREATMENT ○ YES ○ NO
TYPE ____

Hops

VARIETY ____
SPECIFIC PROPERTIES ____
____
____
% AMOUNT ____
ORIGIN/NAME ____

Other Flavorings

TYPE ____
AMOUNT ____
USED FOR ____
ADDED DURING ____

NOTES ____
____
____
____
____
____
____

Brewing Log

DATE BREWED ______

BATCH SIZE ______

TASTING NOTES ______

______

______

BEGINNING SPECIFIC GRAVITY ______

FINAL SPECIFIC GRAVITY ______

______ % ALCOHOL ______

Boil + Mash

TEMPERATURE OF GRAIN ______

TEMPERATURE OF TUN ______

BOIL TIME ______

COOLING TIME & TEMPERATURE ______

Hops added

BOIL TIME ______

COOLING TIME & TEMPERATURE ______

SPECIFIC GRAVITY ______

Yeast added

TEMPERATURE ______

LENGTH OF FERMENT ______

BOTTLING GRAVITY ______

TYPE OF VESSEL ______

PRIMER & AMOUNT ______

Storing and Aging

AGED FOR ______

STORAGE TEMPERATURE ______

NOTES ______

Tasting and Visual Notes

______ OG ______ SRM

______ ABV ______ IBUs

APPEARANCE ______

AROMA ______

FLAVOR ______

FEEL ______

OVERALL ______

WHAT WORKED?

______

WHAT DIDN'T?

______

NAME TYPE
PROPERTIES I'M GOING FOR

FORM
NOTES

FLAVOR/AROMA/PROCESS

Ingredients

Yeast

NAME
MANUFACTURER
LAST CULTURED

Water

pH TREATMENT ○ YES ○ NO
TYPE

Grain

NAME
ORIGIN
TYPE
ROASTED/TOASTED

○ WHEAT ___% ○ CORN ___%
○ BARLEY ___% ○ OATS ___%
○ MALT ___% ○ RICE ___%
○ RYE ___% ○ OTHER ___%

SPECIFIC PROPERTIES

Hops

VARIETY
SPECIFIC PROPERTIES

% AMOUNT
ORIGIN/NAME

Sugar

GRANULATED SUGAR
BROWN SUGAR
HONEY
MAPLE SYRUP
CORN SYRUP
MALT
MOLASSES
OTHER

Other Flavorings

TYPE
AMOUNT
USED FOR
ADDED DURING

NOTES

Brewing Log

DATE BREWED ______

BATCH SIZE ______

TASTING NOTES ______

______

______

BEGINNING SPECIFIC GRAVITY ______

FINAL SPECIFIC GRAVITY ______

______ % ALCOHOL ______

Boil + Mash

TEMPERATURE OF GRAIN ______

TEMPERATURE OF TUN ______

BOIL TIME ______

COOLING TIME & TEMPERATURE ______

Hops added

BOIL TIME ______

COOLING TIME & TEMPERATURE ______

SPECIFIC GRAVITY ______

Yeast added

TEMPERATURE ______

LENGTH OF FERMENT ______

BOTTLING GRAVITY ______

TYPE OF VESSEL ______

PRIMER & AMOUNT ______

Storing and Aging

AGED FOR ______

STORAGE TEMPERATURE ______

NOTES ______

Tasting and Visual Notes

______ OG ______ SRM

______ ABV ______ IBUs

APPEARANCE ______

AROMA ______

FLAVOR ______

FEEL ______

OVERALL ______

WHAT WORKED?

______

WHAT DIDN'T?

______

NAME ____ TYPE ____
PROPERTIES I'M GOING FOR ____
FORM ____
NOTES ____
FLAVOR/AROMA/PROCESS ____

Ingredients

Yeast

NAME ____
MANUFACTURER ____
LAST CULTURED ____

Water

pH TREATMENT ○ YES ○ NO
TYPE ____

Grain

NAME ____
ORIGIN ____
TYPE ____
ROASTED/TOASTED ____

○ WHEAT ____% ○ CORN ____%
○ BARLEY ____% ○ OATS ____%
○ MALT ____% ○ RICE ____%
○ RYE ____% ○ OTHER ____%

SPECIFIC PROPERTIES ____

Hops

VARIETY ____
SPECIFIC PROPERTIES ____
% AMOUNT ____
ORIGIN/NAME ____

Sugar

GRANULATED SUGAR ____
BROWN SUGAR ____
HONEY ____
MAPLE SYRUP ____
CORN SYRUP ____
MALT ____
MOLASSES ____
OTHER ____

Other Flavorings

TYPE ____
AMOUNT ____
USED FOR ____
ADDED DURING ____

NOTES ____

Brewing Log

DATE BREWED ______

BATCH SIZE ______

TASTING NOTES ______

______

______

BEGINNING SPECIFIC GRAVITY ______

FINAL SPECIFIC GRAVITY ______

______ % ALCOHOL ______

Boil + Mash

TEMPERATURE OF GRAIN ______

TEMPERATURE OF TUN ______

BOIL TIME ______

COOLING TIME & TEMPERATURE ______

Hops added

BOIL TIME ______

COOLING TIME & TEMPERATURE ______

SPECIFIC GRAVITY ______

Yeast added

TEMPERATURE ______

LENGTH OF FERMENT ______

BOTTLING GRAVITY ______

TYPE OF VESSEL ______

PRIMER & AMOUNT ______

Storing and Aging

AGED FOR ______

STORAGE TEMPERATURE ______

NOTES ______

Tasting and Visual Notes

______ OG ______ SRM

______ ABV ______ IBUs

APPEARANCE ______

AROMA ______

FLAVOR ______

FEEL ______

OVERALL ______

WHAT WORKED?

______

WHAT DIDN'T?

______

NAME ____ TYPE ____
PROPERTIES I'M GOING FOR ____
FORM ____
NOTES ____
FLAVOR/AROMA/PROCESS ____

Ingredients

Yeast

NAME ____
MANUFACTURER ____
LAST CULTURED ____

Water

pH TREATMENT ○ YES ○ NO
TYPE ____

Grain

NAME ____
ORIGIN ____
TYPE ____
ROASTED/TOASTED ____

○ WHEAT ____%
○ BARLEY ____%
○ MALT ____%
○ RYE ____%
○ CORN ____%
○ OATS ____%
○ RICE ____%
○ OTHER ____%

SPECIFIC PROPERTIES ____

Hops

VARIETY ____
SPECIFIC PROPERTIES ____
% AMOUNT ____
ORIGIN/NAME ____

Sugar

GRANULATED SUGAR ____
BROWN SUGAR ____
HONEY ____
MAPLE SYRUP ____
CORN SYRUP ____
MALT ____
MOLASSES ____
OTHER ____

Other Flavorings

TYPE ____
AMOUNT ____
USED FOR ____
ADDED DURING ____

NOTES ____

Brewing Log

DATE BREWED ______

BATCH SIZE ______

TASTING NOTES ______

BEGINNING SPECIFIC GRAVITY ______

FINAL SPECIFIC GRAVITY ______

______ % ALCOHOL ______

Boil + Mash

TEMPERATURE OF GRAIN ______

TEMPERATURE OF TUN ______

BOIL TIME ______

COOLING TIME & TEMPERATURE ______

Hops added

BOIL TIME ______

COOLING TIME & TEMPERATURE ______

SPECIFIC GRAVITY ______

Yeast added

TEMPERATURE ______

LENGTH OF FERMENT ______

BOTTLING GRAVITY ______

TYPE OF VESSEL ______

PRIMER & AMOUNT ______

Storing and Aging

AGED FOR ______

STORAGE TEMPERATURE ______

NOTES ______

Tasting and Visual Notes

______ OG ______ SRM

______ ABV ______ IBUs

APPEARANCE ______

AROMA ______

FLAVOR ______

FEEL ______

OVERALL ______

WHAT WORKED?

WHAT DIDN'T?

NAME | TYPE
PROPERTIES I'M GOING FOR
FORM
NOTES
FLAVOR/AROMA/PROCESS

Ingredients

Yeast

NAME

MANUFACTURER

LAST CULTURED

Water

pH TREATMENT ○ YES ○ NO

TYPE

Grain

NAME

ORIGIN

TYPE

ROASTED/TOASTED

- ○ WHEAT ___%
- ○ BARLEY ___%
- ○ MALT ___%
- ○ RYE ___%
- ○ CORN ___%
- ○ OATS ___%
- ○ RICE ___%
- ○ OTHER ___%

SPECIFIC PROPERTIES

Hops

VARIETY

SPECIFIC PROPERTIES

% AMOUNT

ORIGIN/NAME

Sugar

GRANULATED SUGAR

BROWN SUGAR

HONEY

MAPLE SYRUP

CORN SYRUP

MALT

MOLASSES

OTHER

Other Flavorings

TYPE

AMOUNT

USED FOR

ADDED DURING

NOTES

Brewing Log

DATE BREWED ______

BATCH SIZE ______

TASTING NOTES ______

______

______

BEGINNING SPECIFIC GRAVITY ______

FINAL SPECIFIC GRAVITY ______

______ % ALCOHOL ______

Boil + Mash

TEMPERATURE OF GRAIN ______

TEMPERATURE OF TUN ______

BOIL TIME ______

COOLING TIME & TEMPERATURE ______

Hops added

BOIL TIME ______

COOLING TIME & TEMPERATURE ______

SPECIFIC GRAVITY ______

Yeast added

TEMPERATURE ______

LENGTH OF FERMENT ______

BOTTLING GRAVITY ______

TYPE OF VESSEL ______

PRIMER & AMOUNT ______

Storing and Aging

AGED FOR ______

STORAGE TEMPERATURE ______

NOTES ______

Tasting and Visual Notes

______ OG ______ SRM

______ ABV ______ IBUs

APPEARANCE ______

AROMA ______

FLAVOR ______

FEEL ______

OVERALL ______

WHAT WORKED?

______

WHAT DIDN'T?

______

NAME TYPE
PROPERTIES I'M GOING FOR
FORM
NOTES
FLAVOR/AROMA/PROCESS

Ingredients

Yeast

NAME
MANUFACTURER
LAST CULTURED

Water

pH TREATMENT ○ YES ○ NO
TYPE

Grain

NAME
ORIGIN
TYPE
ROASTED/TOASTED

- ○ WHEAT ___%
- ○ BARLEY ___%
- ○ MALT ___%
- ○ RYE ___%
- ○ CORN ___%
- ○ OATS ___%
- ○ RICE ___%
- ○ OTHER ___%

SPECIFIC PROPERTIES

Hops

VARIETY
SPECIFIC PROPERTIES
% AMOUNT
ORIGIN/NAME

Sugar

GRANULATED SUGAR
BROWN SUGAR
HONEY
MAPLE SYRUP
CORN SYRUP
MALT
MOLASSES
OTHER

Other Flavorings

TYPE
AMOUNT
USED FOR
ADDED DURING

NOTES

Brewing Log

DATE BREWED ______

BATCH SIZE ______

TASTING NOTES ______

______

______

BEGINNING SPECIFIC GRAVITY ______

FINAL SPECIFIC GRAVITY ______

______ % ALCOHOL ______

Boil + Mash

TEMPERATURE OF GRAIN ______

TEMPERATURE OF TUN ______

BOIL TIME ______

COOLING TIME & TEMPERATURE ______

Hops added

BOIL TIME ______

COOLING TIME & TEMPERATURE ______

SPECIFIC GRAVITY ______

Yeast added

TEMPERATURE ______

LENGTH OF FERMENT ______

BOTTLING GRAVITY ______

TYPE OF VESSEL ______

PRIMER & AMOUNT ______

Storing and Aging

AGED FOR ______

STORAGE TEMPERATURE ______

NOTES ______

Tasting and Visual Notes

______ OG ______ SRM

______ ABV ______ IBUs

APPEARANCE ______

AROMA ______

FLAVOR ______

FEEL ______

OVERALL ______

WHAT WORKED?

______

WHAT DIDN'T?

______

NAME TYPE
PROPERTIES I'M GOING FOR

FORM
NOTES

FLAVOR/AROMA/PROCESS

Ingredients

Yeast

NAME

MANUFACTURER

LAST CULTURED

Water

pH TREATMENT ○ YES ○ NO

TYPE

Grain

NAME

ORIGIN

TYPE

ROASTED/TOASTED

○ WHEAT ____%
○ BARLEY ____%
○ MALT ____%
○ RYE ____%
○ CORN ____%
○ OATS ____%
○ RICE ____%
○ OTHER ____%

SPECIFIC PROPERTIES

Hops

VARIETY

SPECIFIC PROPERTIES

% AMOUNT

ORIGIN/NAME

Sugar

GRANULATED SUGAR

BROWN SUGAR

HONEY

MAPLE SYRUP

CORN SYRUP

MALT

MOLASSES

OTHER

Other Flavorings

TYPE

AMOUNT

USED FOR

ADDED DURING

NOTES

Brewing Log

DATE BREWED ______

BATCH SIZE ______

TASTING NOTES ______

______

______

BEGINNING SPECIFIC GRAVITY ______

FINAL SPECIFIC GRAVITY ______

______ % ALCOHOL ______

Boil + Mash

TEMPERATURE OF GRAIN ______

TEMPERATURE OF TUN ______

BOIL TIME ______

COOLING TIME & TEMPERATURE ______

Hops added

BOIL TIME ______

COOLING TIME & TEMPERATURE ______

SPECIFIC GRAVITY ______

Yeast added

TEMPERATURE ______

LENGTH OF FERMENT ______

BOTTLING GRAVITY ______

TYPE OF VESSEL ______

PRIMER & AMOUNT ______

Storing and Aging

AGED FOR ______

STORAGE TEMPERATURE ______

NOTES ______

Tasting and Visual Notes

______ OG ______ SRM

______ ABV ______ IBUs

APPEARANCE ______

AROMA ______

FLAVOR ______

FEEL ______

OVERALL ______

WHAT WORKED?

______

______

______

WHAT DIDN'T?

______

______

______

NAME | TYPE
PROPERTIES I'M GOING FOR

FORM
NOTES

FLAVOR/AROMA/PROCESS

Ingredients

Yeast

NAME
MANUFACTURER
LAST CULTURED

Water

pH TREATMENT ○ YES ○ NO
TYPE

Grain

NAME
ORIGIN
TYPE
ROASTED/TOASTED

○ WHEAT ___%   ○ CORN ___%
○ BARLEY ___%   ○ OATS ___%
○ MALT ___%   ○ RICE ___%
○ RYE ___%   ○ OTHER ___%

SPECIFIC PROPERTIES

Hops

VARIETY
SPECIFIC PROPERTIES

% AMOUNT
ORIGIN/NAME

Sugar

GRANULATED SUGAR
BROWN SUGAR
HONEY
MAPLE SYRUP
CORN SYRUP
MALT
MOLASSES
OTHER

Other Flavorings

TYPE
AMOUNT
USED FOR
ADDED DURING

NOTES

Brewing Log

DATE BREWED ______________________

BATCH SIZE ______________________

TASTING NOTES ______________________

____

____

BEGINNING SPECIFIC GRAVITY ________

FINAL SPECIFIC GRAVITY ________

______ % ALCOHOL ________

Boil + Mash

TEMPERATURE OF GRAIN ________

TEMPERATURE OF TUN ________

BOIL TIME ________

COOLING TIME & TEMPERATURE ________

Hops added

BOIL TIME ________

COOLING TIME & TEMPERATURE ________

SPECIFIC GRAVITY ________

Yeast added

TEMPERATURE ________

LENGTH OF FERMENT ________

BOTTLING GRAVITY ________

TYPE OF VESSEL ________

PRIMER & AMOUNT ________

Storing and Aging

AGED FOR ________

STORAGE TEMPERATURE ________

NOTES ______________________

Tasting and Visual Notes

______ OG ______ SRM

______ ABV ______ IBUs

APPEARANCE ______________________

AROMA ______________________

FLAVOR ______________________

FEEL ______________________

OVERALL ______________________

WHAT WORKED?

____

____

____

WHAT DIDN'T?

____

____

____

NAME ______ TYPE ______

PROPERTIES I'M GOING FOR ______

FORM ______

NOTES ______

FLAVOR/AROMA/PROCESS ______

Ingredients

Yeast

NAME ______

MANUFACTURER ______

LAST CULTURED ______

Grain

NAME ______

ORIGIN ______

TYPE ______

ROASTED/TOASTED ______

- WHEAT ______%
- BARLEY ______%
- MALT ______%
- RYE ______%
- CORN ______%
- OATS ______%
- RICE ______%
- OTHER ______%

SPECIFIC PROPERTIES ______

Sugar

GRANULATED SUGAR ______

BROWN SUGAR ______

HONEY ______

MAPLE SYRUP ______

CORN SYRUP ______

MALT ______

MOLASSES ______

OTHER ______

Water

pH TREATMENT ○ YES ○ NO

TYPE ______

Hops

VARIETY ______

SPECIFIC PROPERTIES ______

% AMOUNT ______

ORIGIN/NAME ______

Other Flavorings

TYPE ______

AMOUNT ______

USED FOR ______

ADDED DURING ______

NOTES ______

Brewing Log

DATE BREWED ______

BATCH SIZE ______

TASTING NOTES ______

______

______

BEGINNING SPECIFIC GRAVITY ______

FINAL SPECIFIC GRAVITY ______

______ % ALCOHOL ______

Boil + Mash

TEMPERATURE OF GRAIN ______

TEMPERATURE OF TUN ______

BOIL TIME ______

COOLING TIME & TEMPERATURE ______

Hops added

BOIL TIME ______

COOLING TIME & TEMPERATURE ______

SPECIFIC GRAVITY ______

Yeast added

TEMPERATURE ______

LENGTH OF FERMENT ______

BOTTLING GRAVITY ______

TYPE OF VESSEL ______

PRIMER & AMOUNT ______

Storing and Aging

AGED FOR ______

STORAGE TEMPERATURE ______

NOTES ______

Tasting and Visual Notes

______ OG ______ SRM

______ ABV ______ IBUs

APPEARANCE ______

AROMA ______

FLAVOR ______

FEEL ______

OVERALL ______

WHAT WORKED?

______

WHAT DIDN'T?

______

NAME ______ TYPE ______

PROPERTIES I'M GOING FOR ______

FORM ______

NOTES ______

FLAVOR/AROMA/PROCESS ______

Ingredients

Yeast

NAME ______

MANUFACTURER ______

LAST CULTURED ______

Water

pH TREATMENT ○ YES ○ NO

TYPE ______

Grain

NAME ______

ORIGIN ______

TYPE ______

ROASTED/TOASTED ______

○ WHEAT ___% ○ CORN ___%

○ BARLEY ___% ○ OATS ___%

○ MALT ___% ○ RICE ___%

○ RYE ___% ○ OTHER ___%

SPECIFIC PROPERTIES ______

Hops

VARIETY ______

SPECIFIC PROPERTIES ______

% AMOUNT ______

ORIGIN/NAME ______

Sugar

GRANULATED SUGAR ______

BROWN SUGAR ______

HONEY ______

MAPLE SYRUP ______

CORN SYRUP ______

MALT ______

MOLASSES ______

OTHER ______

Other Flavorings

TYPE ______

AMOUNT ______

USED FOR ______

ADDED DURING ______

NOTES ______

Brewing Log

DATE BREWED ____
BATCH SIZE ____
TASTING NOTES ____

BEGINNING SPECIFIC GRAVITY ____
FINAL SPECIFIC GRAVITY ____
____ % ALCOHOL ____

Boil + Mash

TEMPERATURE OF GRAIN ____
TEMPERATURE OF TUN ____
BOIL TIME ____
COOLING TIME & TEMPERATURE ____

Hops added

BOIL TIME ____
COOLING TIME & TEMPERATURE ____
SPECIFIC GRAVITY ____

Yeast added

TEMPERATURE ____
LENGTH OF FERMENT ____
BOTTLING GRAVITY ____
TYPE OF VESSEL ____
PRIMER & AMOUNT ____

Storing and Aging

AGED FOR ____
STORAGE TEMPERATURE ____

NOTES ____

Tasting and Visual Notes

____ OG ____ SRM
____ ABV ____ IBUs

APPEARANCE ____
AROMA ____
FLAVOR ____
FEEL ____
OVERALL ____

WHAT WORKED?

WHAT DIDN'T?

NAME ____ TYPE ____

PROPERTIES I'M GOING FOR ____

FORM ____

NOTES ____

FLAVOR/AROMA/PROCESS ____

Ingredients

Yeast

NAME ____

MANUFACTURER ____

LAST CULTURED ____

Water

pH TREATMENT ○ YES ○ NO

TYPE ____

Grain

NAME ____

ORIGIN ____

TYPE ____

ROASTED/TOASTED ____

- ○ WHEAT ____%
- ○ BARLEY ____%
- ○ MALT ____%
- ○ RYE ____%
- ○ CORN ____%
- ○ OATS ____%
- ○ RICE ____%
- ○ OTHER ____%

SPECIFIC PROPERTIES ____

Hops

VARIETY ____

SPECIFIC PROPERTIES ____

% AMOUNT ____

ORIGIN/NAME ____

Sugar

GRANULATED SUGAR ____

BROWN SUGAR ____

HONEY ____

MAPLE SYRUP ____

CORN SYRUP ____

MALT ____

MOLASSES ____

OTHER ____

Other Flavorings

TYPE ____

AMOUNT ____

USED FOR ____

ADDED DURING ____

NOTES ____

Brewing Log

DATE BREWED ____________

BATCH SIZE ____________

TASTING NOTES ____________

BEGINNING SPECIFIC GRAVITY ____________

FINAL SPECIFIC GRAVITY ____________

______ % ALCOHOL ____________

Boil + Mash

TEMPERATURE OF GRAIN ____________

TEMPERATURE OF TUN ____________

BOIL TIME ____________

COOLING TIME & TEMPERATURE ____________

Hops added

BOIL TIME ____________

COOLING TIME & TEMPERATURE ____________

SPECIFIC GRAVITY ____________

Yeast added

TEMPERATURE ____________

LENGTH OF FERMENT ____________

BOTTLING GRAVITY ____________

TYPE OF VESSEL ____________

PRIMER & AMOUNT ____________

Storing and Aging

AGED FOR ____________

STORAGE TEMPERATURE ____________

NOTES ____________

Tasting and Visual Notes

______ OG ______ SRM

______ ABV ______ IBUs

APPEARANCE ____________

AROMA ____________

FLAVOR ____________

FEEL ____________

OVERALL ____________

WHAT WORKED?

WHAT DIDN'T?

NAME ______ TYPE ______
PROPERTIES I'M GOING FOR ______
______
FORM ______
NOTES ______
______
FLAVOR/AROMA/PROCESS ______

Ingredients

Yeast

NAME ______
MANUFACTURER ______
LAST CULTURED ______

Water

pH TREATMENT ○ YES ○ NO
TYPE ______

Grain

NAME ______
ORIGIN ______
TYPE ______
ROASTED/TOASTED ______

- ○ WHEAT ______%
- ○ BARLEY ______%
- ○ MALT ______%
- ○ RYE ______%
- ○ CORN ______%
- ○ OATS ______%
- ○ RICE ______%
- ○ OTHER ______%

SPECIFIC PROPERTIES ______

Hops

VARIETY ______
SPECIFIC PROPERTIES ______
______
______
% AMOUNT ______
ORIGIN/NAME ______

Sugar

GRANULATED SUGAR ______
BROWN SUGAR ______
HONEY ______
MAPLE SYRUP ______
CORN SYRUP ______
MALT ______
MOLASSES ______
OTHER ______

Other Flavorings

TYPE ______
AMOUNT ______
USED FOR ______
ADDED DURING ______

NOTES ______
______
______
______
______
______
______

Brewing Log

DATE BREWED

BATCH SIZE

TASTING NOTES

BEGINNING SPECIFIC GRAVITY

FINAL SPECIFIC GRAVITY

% ALCOHOL

Boil + Mash

TEMPERATURE OF GRAIN

TEMPERATURE OF TUN

BOIL TIME

COOLING TIME & TEMPERATURE

Hops added

BOIL TIME

COOLING TIME & TEMPERATURE

SPECIFIC GRAVITY

Yeast added

TEMPERATURE

LENGTH OF FERMENT

BOTTLING GRAVITY

TYPE OF VESSEL

PRIMER & AMOUNT

Storing and Aging

AGED FOR

STORAGE TEMPERATURE

NOTES

Tasting and Visual Notes

OG

SRM

ABV

IBUs

APPEARANCE

AROMA

FLAVOR

FEEL

OVERALL

WHAT WORKED?

WHAT DIDN'T?

NAME ____ TYPE ____
PROPERTIES I'M GOING FOR ____
FORM ____
NOTES ____
FLAVOR/AROMA/PROCESS ____

Ingredients

Yeast

NAME ____
MANUFACTURER ____
LAST CULTURED ____

Water

pH TREATMENT ○ YES ○ NO
TYPE ____

Grain

NAME ____
ORIGIN ____
TYPE ____
ROASTED/TOASTED ____

○ WHEAT ____% ○ CORN ____%
○ BARLEY ____% ○ OATS ____%
○ MALT ____% ○ RICE ____%
○ RYE ____% ○ OTHER ____%

SPECIFIC PROPERTIES ____

Hops

VARIETY ____
SPECIFIC PROPERTIES ____
% AMOUNT ____
ORIGIN/NAME ____

Sugar

GRANULATED SUGAR ____
BROWN SUGAR ____
HONEY ____
MAPLE SYRUP ____
CORN SYRUP ____
MALT ____
MOLASSES ____
OTHER ____

Other Flavorings

TYPE ____
AMOUNT ____
USED FOR ____
ADDED DURING ____

NOTES ____

Brewing Log

DATE BREWED

BATCH SIZE

TASTING NOTES

BEGINNING SPECIFIC GRAVITY

FINAL SPECIFIC GRAVITY

% ALCOHOL

Boil + Mash

TEMPERATURE OF GRAIN

TEMPERATURE OF TUN

BOIL TIME

COOLING TIME & TEMPERATURE

Hops added

BOIL TIME

COOLING TIME & TEMPERATURE

SPECIFIC GRAVITY

Yeast added

TEMPERATURE

LENGTH OF FERMENT

BOTTLING GRAVITY

TYPE OF VESSEL

PRIMER & AMOUNT

Storing and Aging

AGED FOR

STORAGE TEMPERATURE

NOTES

Tasting and Visual Notes

OG

SRM

ABV

IBUs

APPEARANCE

AROMA

FLAVOR

FEEL

OVERALL

WHAT WORKED?

WHAT DIDN'T?

NAME | TYPE
PROPERTIES I'M GOING FOR
FORM
NOTES
FLAVOR/AROMA/PROCESS

Ingredients

Yeast

NAME
MANUFACTURER
LAST CULTURED

Water

pH TREATMENT ○ YES ○ NO
TYPE

Grain

NAME
ORIGIN
TYPE
ROASTED/TOASTED

○ WHEAT ____% ○ CORN ____%
○ BARLEY ____% ○ OATS ____%
○ MALT ____% ○ RICE ____%
○ RYE ____% ○ OTHER ____%

SPECIFIC PROPERTIES

Hops

VARIETY
SPECIFIC PROPERTIES
% AMOUNT
ORIGIN/NAME

Sugar

GRANULATED SUGAR
BROWN SUGAR
HONEY
MAPLE SYRUP
CORN SYRUP
MALT
MOLASSES
OTHER

Other Flavorings

TYPE
AMOUNT
USED FOR
ADDED DURING

NOTES

Brewing Log

DATE BREWED

BATCH SIZE

TASTING NOTES

BEGINNING SPECIFIC GRAVITY

FINAL SPECIFIC GRAVITY

% ALCOHOL

Boil + Mash

TEMPERATURE OF GRAIN

TEMPERATURE OF TUN

BOIL TIME

COOLING TIME & TEMPERATURE

Hops added

BOIL TIME

COOLING TIME & TEMPERATURE

SPECIFIC GRAVITY

Yeast added

TEMPERATURE

LENGTH OF FERMENT

BOTTLING GRAVITY

TYPE OF VESSEL

PRIMER & AMOUNT

Storing and Aging

AGED FOR

STORAGE TEMPERATURE

NOTES

Tasting and Visual Notes

OG

SRM

ABV

IBUs

APPEARANCE

AROMA

FLAVOR

FEEL

OVERALL

WHAT WORKED?

WHAT DIDN'T?

NAME ______ TYPE ______

PROPERTIES I'M GOING FOR ______

FORM ______

NOTES ______

FLAVOR/AROMA/PROCESS ______

Ingredients

Yeast

NAME ______

MANUFACTURER ______

LAST CULTURED ______

Water

pH TREATMENT ○ YES ○ NO

TYPE ______

Grain

NAME ______

ORIGIN ______

TYPE ______

ROASTED/TOASTED ______

- ○ WHEAT ____%
- ○ CORN ____%
- ○ BARLEY ____%
- ○ OATS ____%
- ○ MALT ____%
- ○ RICE ____%
- ○ RYE ____%
- ○ OTHER ____%

SPECIFIC PROPERTIES ______

Hops

VARIETY ______

SPECIFIC PROPERTIES ______

% AMOUNT ______

ORIGIN/NAME ______

Sugar

GRANULATED SUGAR ______

BROWN SUGAR ______

HONEY ______

MAPLE SYRUP ______

CORN SYRUP ______

MALT ______

MOLASSES ______

OTHER ______

Other Flavorings

TYPE ______

AMOUNT ______

USED FOR ______

ADDED DURING ______

NOTES ______

Brewing Log

DATE BREWED ____________

BATCH SIZE ____________

TASTING NOTES ____________

____

____

BEGINNING SPECIFIC GRAVITY ____________

FINAL SPECIFIC GRAVITY ____________

______ % ALCOHOL ____________

Boil + Mash

TEMPERATURE OF GRAIN ____________

TEMPERATURE OF TUN ____________

BOIL TIME ____________

COOLING TIME & TEMPERATURE ____________

Hops added

BOIL TIME ____________

COOLING TIME & TEMPERATURE ____________

SPECIFIC GRAVITY ____________

Yeast added

TEMPERATURE ____________

LENGTH OF FERMENT ____________

BOTTLING GRAVITY ____________

TYPE OF VESSEL ____________

PRIMER & AMOUNT ____________

Storing and Aging

AGED FOR ____________

STORAGE TEMPERATURE ____________

NOTES ____________

Tasting and Visual Notes

______ OG ______ SRM

______ ABV ______ IBUs

APPEARANCE ____________

AROMA ____________

FLAVOR ____________

FEEL ____________

OVERALL ____________

WHAT WORKED?

____

____

____

WHAT DIDN'T?

____

____

____

NAME ____ TYPE ____
PROPERTIES I'M GOING FOR ____
FORM ____
NOTES ____
FLAVOR/AROMA/PROCESS ____

Ingredients

Yeast

NAME ____
MANUFACTURER ____
LAST CULTURED ____

Water

pH TREATMENT ○ YES ○ NO
TYPE ____

Grain

NAME ____
ORIGIN ____
TYPE ____
ROASTED/TOASTED ____

○ WHEAT ____%
○ BARLEY ____%
○ MALT ____%
○ RYE ____%
○ CORN ____%
○ OATS ____%
○ RICE ____%
○ OTHER ____%

SPECIFIC PROPERTIES ____

Hops

VARIETY ____
SPECIFIC PROPERTIES ____
% AMOUNT ____
ORIGIN/NAME ____

Sugar

GRANULATED SUGAR ____
BROWN SUGAR ____
HONEY ____
MAPLE SYRUP ____
CORN SYRUP ____
MALT ____
MOLASSES ____
OTHER ____

Other Flavorings

TYPE ____
AMOUNT ____
USED FOR ____
ADDED DURING ____

NOTES ____

Brewing Log

DATE BREWED ______

BATCH SIZE ______

TASTING NOTES ______

BEGINNING SPECIFIC GRAVITY ______

FINAL SPECIFIC GRAVITY ______

______ % ALCOHOL ______

Boil + Mash

TEMPERATURE OF GRAIN ______

TEMPERATURE OF TUN ______

BOIL TIME ______

COOLING TIME & TEMPERATURE ______

Hops added

BOIL TIME ______

COOLING TIME & TEMPERATURE ______

SPECIFIC GRAVITY ______

Yeast added

TEMPERATURE ______

LENGTH OF FERMENT ______

BOTTLING GRAVITY ______

TYPE OF VESSEL ______

PRIMER & AMOUNT ______

Storing and Aging

AGED FOR ______

STORAGE TEMPERATURE ______

NOTES ______

Tasting and Visual Notes

______ OG ______ SRM

______ ABV ______ IBUs

APPEARANCE ______

AROMA ______

FLAVOR ______

FEEL ______

OVERALL ______

WHAT WORKED?

WHAT DIDN'T?

NAME | TYPE

PROPERTIES I'M GOING FOR

FORM

NOTES

FLAVOR/AROMA/PROCESS

Ingredients

Yeast

NAME

MANUFACTURER

LAST CULTURED

Water

pH TREATMENT ○ YES ○ NO

TYPE

Grain

NAME

ORIGIN

TYPE

ROASTED/TOASTED

- ○ WHEAT ____%
- ○ BARLEY ____%
- ○ MALT ____%
- ○ RYE ____%
- ○ CORN ____%
- ○ OATS ____%
- ○ RICE ____%
- ○ OTHER ____%

SPECIFIC PROPERTIES

Hops

VARIETY

SPECIFIC PROPERTIES

% AMOUNT

ORIGIN/NAME

Sugar

GRANULATED SUGAR

BROWN SUGAR

HONEY

MAPLE SYRUP

CORN SYRUP

MALT

MOLASSES

OTHER

Other Flavorings

TYPE

AMOUNT

USED FOR

ADDED DURING

NOTES

Brewing Log

DATE BREWED ______

BATCH SIZE ______

TASTING NOTES ______

______

______

BEGINNING SPECIFIC GRAVITY ______

FINAL SPECIFIC GRAVITY ______

______ % ALCOHOL ______

Boil + Mash

TEMPERATURE OF GRAIN ______

TEMPERATURE OF TUN ______

BOIL TIME ______

COOLING TIME & TEMPERATURE ______

Hops added

BOIL TIME ______

COOLING TIME & TEMPERATURE ______

SPECIFIC GRAVITY ______

Yeast added

TEMPERATURE ______

LENGTH OF FERMENT ______

BOTTLING GRAVITY ______

TYPE OF VESSEL ______

PRIMER & AMOUNT ______

Storing and Aging

AGED FOR ______

STORAGE TEMPERATURE ______

NOTES ______

Tasting and Visual Notes

______ OG ______ SRM

______ ABV ______ IBUs

APPEARANCE ______

AROMA ______

FLAVOR ______

FEEL ______

OVERALL ______

WHAT WORKED?

______

WHAT DIDN'T?

______

NAME ______ TYPE ______
PROPERTIES I'M GOING FOR ______

FORM ______
NOTES ______

FLAVOR/AROMA/PROCESS ______

Ingredients

Yeast

NAME ______
MANUFACTURER ______
LAST CULTURED ______

Water

pH TREATMENT ○ YES ○ NO
TYPE ______

Grain

NAME ______
ORIGIN ______
TYPE ______
ROASTED/TOASTED ______

○ WHEAT ____%   ○ CORN ____%
○ BARLEY ____%   ○ OATS ____%
○ MALT ____%   ○ RICE ____%
○ RYE ____%   ○ OTHER ____%

SPECIFIC PROPERTIES ______

Hops

VARIETY ______
SPECIFIC PROPERTIES ______

% AMOUNT ______
ORIGIN/NAME ______

Sugar

GRANULATED SUGAR ______
BROWN SUGAR ______
HONEY ______
MAPLE SYRUP ______
CORN SYRUP ______
MALT ______
MOLASSES ______
OTHER ______

Other Flavorings

TYPE ______
AMOUNT ______
USED FOR ______
ADDED DURING ______

NOTES ______

Brewing Log

DATE BREWED ______________________

BATCH SIZE ______________________

TASTING NOTES ______________________

BEGINNING SPECIFIC GRAVITY __________

FINAL SPECIFIC GRAVITY __________

______ % ALCOHOL __________

Boil + Mash

TEMPERATURE OF GRAIN __________

TEMPERATURE OF TUN __________

BOIL TIME __________

COOLING TIME & TEMPERATURE __________

Hops added

BOIL TIME __________

COOLING TIME & TEMPERATURE __________

SPECIFIC GRAVITY __________

Yeast added

TEMPERATURE __________

LENGTH OF FERMENT __________

BOTTLING GRAVITY __________

TYPE OF VESSEL __________

PRIMER & AMOUNT __________

Storing and Aging

AGED FOR __________

STORAGE TEMPERATURE __________

NOTES __________

Tasting and Visual Notes

______ OG ______ SRM

______ ABV ______ IBUs

APPEARANCE __________

AROMA __________

FLAVOR __________

FEEL __________

OVERALL __________

WHAT WORKED?

WHAT DIDN'T?

NAME TYPE

PROPERTIES I'M GOING FOR

FORM

NOTES

FLAVOR/AROMA/PROCESS

Ingredients

Yeast

NAME

MANUFACTURER

LAST CULTURED

Water

pH TREATMENT ○ YES ○ NO

TYPE

Grain

NAME

ORIGIN

TYPE

ROASTED/TOASTED

- ○ WHEAT ___%
- ○ BARLEY ___%
- ○ MALT ___%
- ○ RYE ___%
- ○ CORN ___%
- ○ OATS ___%
- ○ RICE ___%
- ○ OTHER ___%

SPECIFIC PROPERTIES

Hops

VARIETY

SPECIFIC PROPERTIES

% AMOUNT

ORIGIN/NAME

Sugar

GRANULATED SUGAR

BROWN SUGAR

HONEY

MAPLE SYRUP

CORN SYRUP

MALT

MOLASSES

OTHER

Other Flavorings

TYPE

AMOUNT

USED FOR

ADDED DURING

NOTES

Brewing Log

DATE BREWED ____________________

BATCH SIZE ____________________

TASTING NOTES ____________________

____

____

BEGINNING SPECIFIC GRAVITY ____________

FINAL SPECIFIC GRAVITY ____________

______ % ALCOHOL ____________

Boil + Mash

TEMPERATURE OF GRAIN ____________

TEMPERATURE OF TUN ____________

BOIL TIME ____________

COOLING TIME & TEMPERATURE ____________

Hops added

BOIL TIME ____________

COOLING TIME & TEMPERATURE ____________

SPECIFIC GRAVITY ____________

Yeast added

TEMPERATURE ____________

LENGTH OF FERMENT ____________

BOTTLING GRAVITY ____________

TYPE OF VESSEL ____________

PRIMER & AMOUNT ____________

Storing and Aging

AGED FOR ____________

STORAGE TEMPERATURE ____________

NOTES ____________________

Tasting and Visual Notes

______ OG ______ SRM

______ ABV ______ IBUs

APPEARANCE ____________________

AROMA ____________________

FLAVOR ____________________

FEEL ____________________

OVERALL ____________________

WHAT WORKED?

____

____

____

WHAT DIDN'T?

____

____

____

NAME ____ TYPE ____

PROPERTIES I'M GOING FOR ____

FORM ____

NOTES ____

FLAVOR/AROMA/PROCESS ____

Ingredients

Yeast

NAME ____

MANUFACTURER ____

LAST CULTURED ____

Grain

NAME ____

ORIGIN ____

TYPE ____

ROASTED/TOASTED ____

- WHEAT ____%
- BARLEY ____%
- MALT ____%
- RYE ____%
- CORN ____%
- OATS ____%
- RICE ____%
- OTHER ____%

SPECIFIC PROPERTIES ____

Sugar

GRANULATED SUGAR ____

BROWN SUGAR ____

HONEY ____

MAPLE SYRUP ____

CORN SYRUP ____

MALT ____

MOLASSES ____

OTHER ____

Water

pH TREATMENT ○ YES ○ NO

TYPE ____

Hops

VARIETY ____

SPECIFIC PROPERTIES ____

% AMOUNT ____

ORIGIN/NAME ____

Other Flavorings

TYPE ____

AMOUNT ____

USED FOR ____

ADDED DURING ____

NOTES ____

Brewing Log

DATE BREWED ______________________

BATCH SIZE ______________________

TASTING NOTES ______________________

____

____

BEGINNING SPECIFIC GRAVITY ________

FINAL SPECIFIC GRAVITY ________

______ % ALCOHOL ________

Boil + Mash

TEMPERATURE OF GRAIN ______________

TEMPERATURE OF TUN ______________

BOIL TIME ______________

COOLING TIME & TEMPERATURE ______________

Hops added

BOIL TIME ______________

COOLING TIME & TEMPERATURE ______________

SPECIFIC GRAVITY ______________

Yeast added

TEMPERATURE ______________

LENGTH OF FERMENT ______________

BOTTLING GRAVITY ______________

TYPE OF VESSEL ______________

PRIMER & AMOUNT ______________

Storing and Aging

AGED FOR ______________

STORAGE TEMPERATURE ______________

NOTES ______________________

Tasting and Visual Notes

______ OG ______ SRM

______ ABV ______ IBUs

APPEARANCE ______________________

AROMA ______________________

FLAVOR ______________________

FEEL ______________________

OVERALL ______________________

WHAT WORKED?

____

____

____

WHAT DIDN'T?

____

____

____

NAME ______ TYPE ______
PROPERTIES I'M GOING FOR ______
FORM ______
NOTES ______
FLAVOR/AROMA/PROCESS ______

Ingredients

Yeast

NAME ______
MANUFACTURER ______
LAST CULTURED ______

Water

pH TREATMENT ○ YES ○ NO
TYPE ______

Grain

NAME ______
ORIGIN ______
TYPE ______
ROASTED/TOASTED ______

○ WHEAT ____% ○ CORN ____%
○ BARLEY ____% ○ OATS ____%
○ MALT ____% ○ RICE ____%
○ RYE ____% ○ OTHER ____%

SPECIFIC PROPERTIES ______

Hops

VARIETY ______
SPECIFIC PROPERTIES ______
% AMOUNT ______
ORIGIN/NAME ______

Sugar

GRANULATED SUGAR ______
BROWN SUGAR ______
HONEY ______
MAPLE SYRUP ______
CORN SYRUP ______
MALT ______
MOLASSES ______
OTHER ______

Other Flavorings

TYPE ______
AMOUNT ______
USED FOR ______
ADDED DURING ______

NOTES ______

Brewing Log

DATE BREWED ______________________

BATCH SIZE ______________________

TASTING NOTES ______________________

____

____

BEGINNING SPECIFIC GRAVITY ________

FINAL SPECIFIC GRAVITY ________

________ % ALCOHOL ________

Boil + Mash

TEMPERATURE OF GRAIN ________

TEMPERATURE OF TUN ________

BOIL TIME ________

COOLING TIME & TEMPERATURE ________

Hops added

BOIL TIME ________

COOLING TIME & TEMPERATURE ________

SPECIFIC GRAVITY ________

Yeast added

TEMPERATURE ________

LENGTH OF FERMENT ________

BOTTLING GRAVITY ________

TYPE OF VESSEL ________

PRIMER & AMOUNT ________

Storing and Aging

AGED FOR ________

STORAGE TEMPERATURE ________

NOTES ______________________

Tasting and Visual Notes

________ OG ________ SRM

________ ABV ________ IBUs

APPEARANCE ______________________

AROMA ______________________

FLAVOR ______________________

FEEL ______________________

OVERALL ______________________

WHAT WORKED?

____

____

____

WHAT DIDN'T?

____

____

____

NAME TYPE

PROPERTIES I'M GOING FOR

FORM

NOTES

FLAVOR/AROMA/PROCESS

Ingredients

Yeast

NAME

MANUFACTURER

LAST CULTURED

Water

pH TREATMENT YES NO

TYPE

Grain

NAME

ORIGIN

TYPE

ROASTED/TOASTED

- WHEAT ____%
- BARLEY ____%
- MALT ____%
- RYE ____%
- CORN ____%
- OATS ____%
- RICE ____%
- OTHER ____%

SPECIFIC PROPERTIES

Hops

VARIETY

SPECIFIC PROPERTIES

% AMOUNT

ORIGIN/NAME

Sugar

GRANULATED SUGAR

BROWN SUGAR

HONEY

MAPLE SYRUP

CORN SYRUP

MALT

MOLASSES

OTHER

Other Flavorings

TYPE

AMOUNT

USED FOR

ADDED DURING

NOTES

Brewing Log

DATE BREWED ______

BATCH SIZE ______

TASTING NOTES ______

______

______

BEGINNING SPECIFIC GRAVITY ______

FINAL SPECIFIC GRAVITY ______

______ % ALCOHOL ______

Boil + Mash

TEMPERATURE OF GRAIN ______

TEMPERATURE OF TUN ______

BOIL TIME ______

COOLING TIME & TEMPERATURE ______

Hops added

BOIL TIME ______

COOLING TIME & TEMPERATURE ______

SPECIFIC GRAVITY ______

Yeast added

TEMPERATURE ______

LENGTH OF FERMENT ______

BOTTLING GRAVITY ______

TYPE OF VESSEL ______

PRIMER & AMOUNT ______

Storing and Aging

AGED FOR ______

STORAGE TEMPERATURE ______

NOTES ______

Tasting and Visual Notes

______ OG ______ SRM

______ ABV ______ IBUs

APPEARANCE ______

AROMA ______

FLAVOR ______

FEEL ______

OVERALL ______

WHAT WORKED?

______

______

______

WHAT DIDN'T?

______

______

______

NAME TYPE

PROPERTIES I'M GOING FOR

FORM

NOTES

FLAVOR/AROMA/PROCESS

Ingredients

Yeast

NAME

MANUFACTURER

LAST CULTURED

Water

pH TREATMENT YES NO

TYPE

Grain

NAME

ORIGIN

TYPE

ROASTED/TOASTED

WHEAT ____%

BARLEY ____%

MALT ____%

RYE ____%

CORN ____%

OATS ____%

RICE ____%

OTHER ____%

SPECIFIC PROPERTIES

Hops

VARIETY

SPECIFIC PROPERTIES

% AMOUNT

ORIGIN/NAME

Sugar

GRANULATED SUGAR

BROWN SUGAR

HONEY

MAPLE SYRUP

CORN SYRUP

MALT

MOLASSES

OTHER

Other Flavorings

TYPE

AMOUNT

USED FOR

ADDED DURING

NOTES

Brewing Log

DATE BREWED ______

BATCH SIZE ______

TASTING NOTES ______

______

______

BEGINNING SPECIFIC GRAVITY ______

FINAL SPECIFIC GRAVITY ______

______ % ALCOHOL ______

Boil + Mash

TEMPERATURE OF GRAIN ______

TEMPERATURE OF TUN ______

BOIL TIME ______

COOLING TIME & TEMPERATURE ______

Hops added

BOIL TIME ______

COOLING TIME & TEMPERATURE ______

SPECIFIC GRAVITY ______

Yeast added

TEMPERATURE ______

LENGTH OF FERMENT ______

BOTTLING GRAVITY ______

TYPE OF VESSEL ______

PRIMER & AMOUNT ______

Storing and Aging

AGED FOR ______

STORAGE TEMPERATURE ______

NOTES ______

Tasting and Visual Notes

______ OG ______ SRM

______ ABV ______ IBUs

APPEARANCE ______

AROMA ______

FLAVOR ______

FEEL ______

OVERALL ______

WHAT WORKED?

______

______

______

WHAT DIDN'T?

______

______

______

NAME ____________ TYPE ____________

PROPERTIES I'M GOING FOR ____________

FORM ____________

NOTES ____________

FLAVOR/AROMA/PROCESS ____________

Ingredients

Yeast

NAME ____________

MANUFACTURER ____________

LAST CULTURED ____________

Water

pH TREATMENT ○ YES ○ NO

TYPE ____________

Grain

NAME ____________

ORIGIN ____________

TYPE ____________

ROASTED/TOASTED ____________

○ WHEAT ____% ○ CORN ____%

○ BARLEY ____% ○ OATS ____%

○ MALT ____% ○ RICE ____%

○ RYE ____% ○ OTHER ____%

SPECIFIC PROPERTIES ____________

Hops

VARIETY ____________

SPECIFIC PROPERTIES ____________

% AMOUNT ____________

ORIGIN/NAME ____________

Sugar

GRANULATED SUGAR ____________

BROWN SUGAR ____________

HONEY ____________

MAPLE SYRUP ____________

CORN SYRUP ____________

MALT ____________

MOLASSES ____________

OTHER ____________

Other Flavorings

TYPE ____________

AMOUNT ____________

USED FOR ____________

ADDED DURING ____________

NOTES ____________

Brewing Log

DATE BREWED ______

BATCH SIZE ______

TASTING NOTES ______

______

______

BEGINNING SPECIFIC GRAVITY ______

FINAL SPECIFIC GRAVITY ______

______ % ALCOHOL ______

Boil + Mash

TEMPERATURE OF GRAIN ______

TEMPERATURE OF TUN ______

BOIL TIME ______

COOLING TIME & TEMPERATURE ______

Hops added

BOIL TIME ______

COOLING TIME & TEMPERATURE ______

SPECIFIC GRAVITY ______

Yeast added

TEMPERATURE ______

LENGTH OF FERMENT ______

BOTTLING GRAVITY ______

TYPE OF VESSEL ______

PRIMER & AMOUNT ______

Storing and Aging

AGED FOR ______

STORAGE TEMPERATURE ______

NOTES ______

Tasting and Visual Notes

______ OG ______ SRM

______ ABV ______ IBUs

APPEARANCE ______

AROMA ______

FLAVOR ______

FEEL ______

OVERALL ______

WHAT WORKED?

______

WHAT DIDN'T?

______

NAME ______ TYPE ______

PROPERTIES I'M GOING FOR ______

FORM ______

NOTES ______

FLAVOR/AROMA/PROCESS ______

Ingredients

Yeast

NAME ______

MANUFACTURER ______

LAST CULTURED ______

Water

pH TREATMENT ○ YES ○ NO

TYPE ______

Grain

NAME ______

ORIGIN ______

TYPE ______

ROASTED/TOASTED ______

○ WHEAT ____% ○ CORN ____%

○ BARLEY ____% ○ OATS ____%

○ MALT ____% ○ RICE ____%

○ RYE ____% ○ OTHER ____%

SPECIFIC PROPERTIES ______

Hops

VARIETY ______

SPECIFIC PROPERTIES ______

% AMOUNT ______

ORIGIN/NAME ______

Sugar

GRANULATED SUGAR ______

BROWN SUGAR ______

HONEY ______

MAPLE SYRUP ______

CORN SYRUP ______

MALT ______

MOLASSES ______

OTHER ______

Other Flavorings

TYPE ______

AMOUNT ______

USED FOR ______

ADDED DURING ______

NOTES ______

Brewing Log

DATE BREWED ______

BATCH SIZE ______

TASTING NOTES ______

______

______

BEGINNING SPECIFIC GRAVITY ______

FINAL SPECIFIC GRAVITY ______

______ % ALCOHOL ______

Boil + Mash

TEMPERATURE OF GRAIN ______

TEMPERATURE OF TUN ______

BOIL TIME ______

COOLING TIME & TEMPERATURE ______

Hops added

BOIL TIME ______

COOLING TIME & TEMPERATURE ______

SPECIFIC GRAVITY ______

Yeast added

TEMPERATURE ______

LENGTH OF FERMENT ______

BOTTLING GRAVITY ______

TYPE OF VESSEL ______

PRIMER & AMOUNT ______

Storing and Aging

AGED FOR ______

STORAGE TEMPERATURE ______

NOTES ______

Tasting and Visual Notes

______ OG ______ SRM

______ ABV ______ IBUs

APPEARANCE ______

AROMA ______

FLAVOR ______

FEEL ______

OVERALL ______

WHAT WORKED?

______

______

______

WHAT DIDN'T?

______

______

______

NAME ______ TYPE ______

PROPERTIES I'M GOING FOR ______

FORM ______

NOTES ______

FLAVOR/AROMA/PROCESS ______

Ingredients

Yeast

NAME ______

MANUFACTURER ______

LAST CULTURED ______

Water

pH TREATMENT ○ YES ○ NO

TYPE ______

Grain

NAME ______

ORIGIN ______

TYPE ______

ROASTED/TOASTED ______

○ WHEAT ____% ○ CORN ____%

○ BARLEY ____% ○ OATS ____%

○ MALT ____% ○ RICE ____%

○ RYE ____% ○ OTHER ____%

SPECIFIC PROPERTIES ______

Hops

VARIETY ______

SPECIFIC PROPERTIES ______

% AMOUNT ______

ORIGIN/NAME ______

Sugar

GRANULATED SUGAR ______

BROWN SUGAR ______

HONEY ______

MAPLE SYRUP ______

CORN SYRUP ______

MALT ______

MOLASSES ______

OTHER ______

Other Flavorings

TYPE ______

AMOUNT ______

USED FOR ______

ADDED DURING ______

NOTES ______

Brewing Log

DATE BREWED ______

BATCH SIZE ______

TASTING NOTES ______

______

______

BEGINNING SPECIFIC GRAVITY ______

FINAL SPECIFIC GRAVITY ______

______ % ALCOHOL ______

Boil + Mash

TEMPERATURE OF GRAIN ______

TEMPERATURE OF TUN ______

BOIL TIME ______

COOLING TIME & TEMPERATURE ______

Hops added

BOIL TIME ______

COOLING TIME & TEMPERATURE ______

SPECIFIC GRAVITY ______

Yeast added

TEMPERATURE ______

LENGTH OF FERMENT ______

BOTTLING GRAVITY ______

TYPE OF VESSEL ______

PRIMER & AMOUNT ______

Storing and Aging

AGED FOR ______

STORAGE TEMPERATURE ______

NOTES ______

Tasting and Visual Notes

______ OG ______ SRM

______ ABV ______ IBUs

APPEARANCE ______

AROMA ______

FLAVOR ______

FEEL ______

OVERALL ______

WHAT WORKED?

______

WHAT DIDN'T?

______